4.50

I Am Not Ashamed

ADVICE TO TIMOTHY

D. MARTYN LLOYD-JONES

edited by Christopher Catherwood

BAKER BOOK HOUSE
Grand Rapids, Michigan 49506

Copyright © 1986 by Mrs. Bethan Lloyd-Jones

Published by Baker Books
a division of Baker Book House Company
P.O. Box 6287, Grand Rapids, MI 49516-6287

ISBN: 0-8010-5634-9

Sixth printing, April 1996

Printed in the United States of America

Contents

Preface

by Christopher Catherwood
(author of *Five Evangelical Leaders*)

'Logic on fire! Eloquent reason!' These were the two expressions used by my grandfather, Dr Martyn Lloyd-Jones, in his classic work *Preaching and Preachers* to describe what preaching was all about. They describe very accurately the style of his evangelistic sermons, delivered in Westminster Chapel during 1964, on 2 Timothy.

Martyn Lloyd-Jones was always affectionately known as 'the Doctor' and it was a most fitting appellation. To start with, he was a doctor of medicine, not of theology, and it was this that gave his evangelism a unique cutting edge. He was trained at St. Bartholomew's Hospital – Bart's – under the eminent physician Lord Horder, gaining his MB and BS in 1921, with the MD and MRCP following not long afterwards. In 1923, aged only twenty-three, he became Horder's chief clinical assistant. Horder was the most brilliant diagnostician of his time, and instilled his way of thinking into all his pupils. He rewarded his star pupil – Martyn Lloyd-Jones – with his own copy of Jevon's famous book: *Principles of Science – a treatise on logical and scientific method*. In 1927, however, Dr Lloyd-Jones returned to his native Wales, in order to become the minister of a church in Aberavon. God, he felt, had called him to preach the gospel. In 1938 he was made minister of Westminster Chapel in London, where he remained until 1968.

But although he had abandoned what promised to be a highly successful medical career, he remained a physician in his way of thought until the end of his life. The only difference was that he was now a doctor of souls instead of diseases. The principles which he had learned under Horder transferred themselves from the hospital ward into the sermons. To the Doctor, Christianity was above all reasonable. His fellow Welshmen, he discovered early on in Aberavon, could easily be moved, but their minds would be unchanged. So he proclaimed his message as one that was 'very relevant and urgently important.' He deliberately avoided the flamboyant pulpit style so prevalent in his day. Christianity was God's truth, and the only answer both to the world's problems and to those of everyone who listened to what it claimed.

For, in the same way that his patients at Bart's had been sick, so too were men and women without God. What they needed was a cure – in this case salvation through Jesus Christ on the cross. But first of all, people had to be helped to see their need. So the Doctor would always start with the world as everyone could see it – lost and helpless, without a hope. Man, as always, had tried various solutions of his own, but these had failed. What, then, could be done? What, indeed, was the root cause of the problem? Well, it was that men and women were sinners, in rebellion against God. The time had come for the real diagnoses, and to reject the quack remedies on offer. With the same careful logic that he had learned under Horder, the Doctor would show his listeners the evidence that God's offer of salvation through his son Jesus Christ was the only way.

It is this methodology that makes Martyn Lloyd-Jones' sermons so distinctive and the sermons in this book so special. Other facets of his medical training appear in the way in which he deals with Timothy's temperament – 'Timid Timothy' as he is often known. As my grandfather demonstrates, while temperament and personality are important, there is no such thing as a Christian type. The gospel is for everyone, whatever their make-up. Above all, the message is as true in the twentieth century as when Paul wrote his letter to Timothy from the prison cell in Rome. Paul was not ashamed of

the good news of Jesus Christ and nor are God's people
today.

Balsham,
Cambridgeshire,
June 1985

Explanatory note:
The originals of the sermons contained here were transcribed
at the time by his secretary, Mrs Burney. When he died, my
grandfather left his family these transcripts, and it is from
them that this book has been edited for publication. In this
task I have been greatly helped both by my grandmother,
Bethan Lloyd-Jones, and by my mother, the Doctor's elder
daughter Elizabeth Catherwood. To each of them I am
immensely thankful. We have stuck closely to the method
used by Martyn Lloyd-Jones in his lifetime, such as removing
repetition not necessary for a book at the beginning of each
sermon. Otherwise, what you read here is very much as it was
preached in Westminster Chapel in Spring 1964. I would also
wish to express my usual warm appreciation to my agent
Edward England and to my editor at Hodder and Stoughton,
David Wavre, for all their help and advice.

Chapter One

SUNDAY EVENING SERMON
12th April 1964

The Problem of Life

For the which cause I also suffer these things: nevertheless I am not ashamed: for I know whom I have believed, and am persuaded that he is able to keep that which I have committed unto him against that day (2 Tim. 1:12).

In starting, I emphasise that particular verse, but you will notice, if you read the rest of the chapter, that that verse is a part of a larger statement. There is, therefore, a sense in which it is almost ridiculous to take just that one verse out of its context and its setting. And yet I do so because it will serve us, perhaps best of all, as a kind of introduction to the whole theme which is handled by the great apostle in this chapter. For here, in this particular verse, Paul makes one of those grand, moving statements which are so characteristic of him and of his writing – one of those profound elemental statements in which he puts before us the great essentials of the Christian faith and what it means to a man who truly believes it.

I call your attention to this statement and the whole argument which is involved in it, because it seems to me that it is of such importance to us at this very time in which we live. You see the great problem that is raised here is the problem of how to live, how to live in a victorious manner, how to face life with all its uncertainty and attendant problems and yet to triumph and to prevail; in other words how to live and master life instead of being mastered by it. But the apostle is incapable of considering that vital theme, or indeed any other theme, without bringing in the whole of the gospel. The two things, as I am going to try to show you invariably and inevitably go together. So the two leading ideas here are how to master life, and the true nature of the gospel.

Now, the test of any teaching, or of any philosophy with respect to life, is, in the last analysis, does it work? Does it help you? Does it really make a difference? We can all philosophise, we can all express our opinions and make our statements, but, after all, the test of the value of all these statements is, are they true? Do they do what we claim for them? Are they really what we stand in need of? Now, the world today is full of all sorts of teachings and theories and ideas, but the question is, do they work? And, especially, do they help when you test them against every conceivable eventuality?

The claim which we make for the Christian gospel is that it works, that it is not a mere theory, but that it is something which really does what it claims to do, that it enables a man to live in a real sense in this world. That is the claim we make for the gospel, but we go further and say that it, and it alone, does that.

Now, this is sometimes regarded by people as being arrogant, but it is not, because if it is true it is not arrogant. And I am claiming that it is true, and I am going to try to demonstrate this. The gospel claims that it is unique. It does not put itself into series with other teachings or with other religions. It says it is absolutely unique, entirely on its own. That is the great claim which is made right through the Bible, Old Testament and New Testament, and when the Christian Church ceases to make that claim, she might as well go out of business, and cease to call herself Christian, because there will be nothing unique left. The claim we make is the one the apostle Peter put to the authorities right at the very beginning of the Church – '. . . there is none other name under heaven given among men, whereby we must be saved' (Acts 4:12). There is only one saviour, there is only one salvation, there is only one teaching that really does enable us to meet all the possible eventualities in this life and in this world.

That, then, is the claim, and Paul put it here in the form of his own experience, which gives a kind of additional value to it. He was writing to his young disciple Timothy, because Timothy was somewhat depressed and unhappy. The apostle did not write merely for the sake of writing, but because he knew of Timothy's state at the time. Timothy, by nature and by temperament, was obviously a man who was easily discouraged and easily depressed. There are people like that. We are not all the same, we are born different and must recognise that. The Christian gospel does so – it recognises that we are different by nature, and Timothy, who was clearly a depressive, if you may so like to describe it, was particularly worried by the fact that the great apostle was a prisoner. It is very important that we too should be aware of that. You can read great statements like this and say, 'Ah well, that is all right, I read statements like that in literature, I find the poets making remarkable statements at times.' But, the poets do not always speak like that; there are times when they cannot do so. The poet has to be in a particular mood, or in particular circumstances, and he is dependent in a sense upon his own moods and feelings and surroundings; but the Christian is not. Here is the apostle in the worst conceivable conditions: he is in prison, he does not know when he may be put to death, everything is against him, and yet this is the way in which he writes; in spite of all these things, he makes this resounding statement, 'I am not ashamed: for I know whom I have believed, and am persuaded that he is able to keep that which I have committed unto him against that day.' There is this tremendous note of triumph, a note of overcoming, in spite of his terrible circumstances.

Now, the apostle puts this before us in what is a very characteristic manner and I must call attention to the way in which he does so. It is to me an increasing source of joy and of thrill that he puts it in this way. 'I am appointed a preacher,' he says, 'and an apostle, and a teacher of the Gentiles. For the which cause' – because I am this – 'I also suffer these things'.

I am in prison, he says, simply because I am a preacher. If I were not preaching this gospel I would not be here, if I were still a Pharisee I would not be here either. I am in prison, I am suffering these things – and he was really suffering – for that reason. So he makes his statement, 'I also suffer . . . nevertheless'. That is it! And there comes the whole of the gospel. Though I am suffering, 'nevertheless I am not ashamed'. His letters are full of this. He says in writing to the Romans 'We . . . rejoice in hope of the glory of God. And not only so, but we glory in tribulations' (Rom. 5:2–3). Now that is typical Christianity, the essence of the Christian teaching. Let me put it like this to you. Christianity, in a sense is in this one word – 'nevertheless', this protest, this rising up above it all: 'nevertheless I am not ashamed'.

Now, I suggest to you that this is the test which we ultimately apply to any view of life that we may chance to hold, and I commend that question to you before we go any further. Are you living life like that? Is there this 'nevertheless' in your life and in your experience? Are you able to look at your circumstances and conditions at their blackest and darkest and starkest, and then say, 'Yes, there they are . . . nevertheless!' Is that your condition?

The question, then, before us is what enabled the apostle to speak like this? How can we all live like this? Is not that the great quest? Is not that the thing we are all concerned about? We live in a difficult world, a gainsaying world that is against us in so many ways, and then there are trials and troubles and problems – illness, accident, death, sorrow. These things come and you never know when. This is the great art of living, is it not, that you can face them all and go through them all saying, 'nevertheless', as the great apostle was able to do. This is what Christianity offers; this is essential Christianity.

What, therefore, was the secret that enabled Paul to do it? What can enable us to do the same? There are many, no doubt, who would suggest that the answer to that question is quite a simple one. 'Of course . . .' they would say, 'there is no problem there. The apostle wrote like that because he just happened to be a man of that sort. You were saying just now that we have different temperaments and there are those who have the hopeful, optimistic, sanguine temperament. We all know them, they are the opposite of the depressive type, the Timothy type, who always see the difficulties and are always full of forebodings. There is this other type of man. You remember them during the two world wars; it did not matter how many battles we lost, or how many things went wrong, these men still came up smiling, saying that everything would be all right. They had no grounds for saying so but they were just like that, born optimistic, always seeing the bright side, always seeing the silver lining! And no doubt,' they would say, 'your apostle was a man of that sort – like a cork, irrepressible, always coming up to the surface again, nothing could keep him down – a man who just happened to have been born like that.'

Well, that is a very attractive and interesting theory but, of course, it is entirely wrong. This is not just my opinion, I can prove what I am saying. We happen to know a great deal about the apostle Paul, and if there is one thing we can say with confidence about him, it is that he was not a born optimist. He was a natural pessimist. He was a very sensitive and highly strung man, one who could be easily discouraged. He tells us this himself, we need not theorise about it. He tells the Corinthians 'For when we came into Macedonia, our flesh had no rest, but we were troubled on every side; without were fightings, within were fears.' He went to Corinth the first time 'in weakness, fear, and much trembling'. A very sensitive man, sensitive to criticism, who could be depressed when people were unkind to him and said unkind things about him. That is this great apostle by nature. He is the exact opposite of the buoyant extrovert, the man who always sees the bright side of everything. Paul was not that sort of man, and he does not write as he does to Timothy because he is a born optimist.

And we can thank God that that is not the explanation, because if the gospel of Jesus Christ is something that can only make born optimists write like this, then it has nothing to give the pessimist, and so many of us are natural pessimists. If the gospel, therefore, cannot make any sort of man write like this, it is no gospel. But the glory of the gospel is that it can take hold of a man of any type of temperament or psychology conceivable and enable him to speak in this manner. It can take even a man like Timothy, and, when it really comes home to him, it can enable him to do exactly the same thing as the great apostle.

Now that, I say, is the special glory of this gospel. It does not matter what your temperament is, it does not matter what your psychology is, nothing matters except the power of the gospel. You see, the gospel does not depend upon us, but upon the power of God. This is the first great principle, therefore, and I emphasise it for this reason. There are clever people today who say, 'Well now, I know there are some people with the religious complex and the religious tempera-ment. All right, let them have it if they want it, but let them not say that we all need it.' My dear friend, I am not talking about complexes, what I am saying is this. You want to triumph over life, do you not, you want to be able to be exultant in the midst of the storm, you would like to be able to rejoice in tribulations? I assure you that the gospel can enable you to do so. Whatever your temperament, whatever your nature, whatever your upbringing – whether you are clever or whether you are not, it does not matter; the gospel is 'the power of God unto salvation'. It does not depend upon us. That is the glory of it! It is a miracle. It gives a man a new birth, it makes a new man of him, and therefore what he is by nature is not the final determining factor.

And then I imagine somebody else bringing forward another suggestion and saying, 'I wonder whether it is that the apostle had become a devotee and a follower of Stoicism, a philosophy that was very popular at that time.' The Stoics are mentioned in Acts where in chapter 17 we read that Paul preached in Athens to a congregation of Stoics and Epicureans. They were very interesting and thoughtful people. The Epicurean was a man who did not think very much – at least the result of his thinking was that the less one thought the better. The thing to do was to enjoy yourself, and if you wanted to enjoy yourself you should not think too much, but rather give yourself to pleasure.

But the Stoic did not take that view. The Stoic was a serious and thoughtful man, an honest one who believed in facing the facts of life. Having done so, he had come to the conclusion that life is a difficult business and a hard task, and that there is only one way of going through with it and that is that you must exercise a firm discipline upon yourself. Life, said the Stoic, will come and attack you, it will batter you and beat you, and the great art of living, he said, is to remain standing on your feet. And the only way to do that is to brace back your shoulders, to set a firm upper lip, to go in for the philosophy of courage, and say, 'I am going to be a man!'

That attitude was very popular in the last war. 'Britain can take it'; 'London can take it'. That is typical Stoicism. You just decide to say, 'No, Hitler is not going to get us down!' That was the typical cockney reaction, was it not? All right, it is very useful when you are at war, but it is not Christianity – it is Stoicism. You just decide that you are not going to give in, you are not going to be defeated; whatever may happen to you, you are still standing, you are going on and you will stick it to the end. The philosophy of grit, the philosophy of courage, the philosophy of the stiff upper lip.

Now, that was a popular teaching in the days of the apostle Paul also, so someone may very well say that the apostle had undoubtedly adopted it, he had become a Stoic, and, therefore, though he was in prison with everything as it were against him, he was not cowed. He was like the poet who said, 'My head is bloody, but unbowed,' I go on. 'I am the master of my fate, I am the captain of my soul.' No, that is not what upheld Paul, and I can show you the difference very easily.

Stoicism, as I have been showing you in defining it – and I am not here to denounce it but to be fair to it – Stoicism on the natural human level is a wonderful thing, but it is not Christianity, and for this reason. Stoicism is the philosophy of resignation, the philosophy of 'putting up with it', of 'sticking it', of refusing to give in. But it is always negative, whereas the very essence of the apostle's statement is positive. The Stoic is never a man who is full of rejoicing, but Paul is full of rejoicing. 'Nevertheless', he says, 'I am not ashamed.' Timothy, what is the matter with you? My dear fellow, he says, do not be sorry for me, and do not be sorry for yourself. Look here, 'be thou partaker of the afflictions of the gospel according to the power of God; who hath saved us'. 'I am not ashamed' – why not? – 'because I know whom I have believed'.

You see this is the man who on one occasion was in another prison with his travelling companion Silas in Philippi. They had been arrested and thrown into the innermost prison. They had done no wrong whatsoever, the authorities were absolutely unjust. But there they were, in the inner prison with their feet fast in the stocks. There were many other prisoners in the prison but there was something different about these two men Paul and Silas. What was it? 'At midnight', we are told, 'Paul and Silas prayed and sang praises unto God.' That is the sort of thing a Stoic has never done and never can do. The Stoic can stick it, he will not whimper and complain and run away, the Stoic can be a man, he is full of courage and he will go through with it. Yes, but he never sings! He does not know what it is to sing. He does not know what it is to be 'more than conqueror'. He just manages to get to the end without falling, but he does not march triumphantly singing as he goes along, rejoicing in the midst of tribulation.

Shall I try to show the difference between Stoicism and Christianity to you by giving you two quotations. I take my first quotation from the poet John Dryden. This is typical Stoicism and a perfect expression of its philosophy:

Since every man who lives is born to die,
And none can know sincere felicity,
With equal mind, what happens, let us bear,
Nor joy nor grieve too much for things beyond our care.
Like pilgrims to the appointed place we tend;
The world's an inn and death the journey's end.

Do you see it? That is typical Stoicism. Let me analyse it for you.

'Since every man who lives is born to die.' I told you, did I not, that the Stoic is a thinking man, not one who turns his back upon life. He faces life and he starts with this elementary proposition: 'every man who lives is born – what for? Well, to die.' To die! There are some foolish people in the world who do not start with that. There are flippant people who do not start with the fact that they have got to die. Now the Stoic is wise enough to see it. He says, 'You know the moment we start living we start dying. There was a baby born a second ago and you say, "There, at any rate, is somebody who has started living." I am equally entitled to say that "there is someone who has started dying". Life is a journey. There is an entry and an exit, and the moment you are in you know you have got to go out.' The Stoic realises that and he faces it. 'Every man who lives is born to die.'

What else? Dryden says, 'none can know sincere felicity'. What he means is that there is no such thing in this life and in this world as complete and entire happiness – sincere, unmixed felicity and pleasure. The Stoic is a very wise man. There is no such thing as a perpetual round of happiness and joy in this world, he says. I know many films and plays may tell you that there is, and you see it acted on your television screens. But it is not true. 'Life is real, life is earnest' and there are problems and trials and tribulations. There is never such a thing as absolute happiness; there is always a fly in the ointment. Nobody has ever been completely and perfectly happy: 'none can know sincere felicity'.

If that is so, then what do we do? Here is the essential philosophy of Stoicism. 'With equal mind, what happens, let us bear.' You see it is the philosophy of the 'even mind', of the even keel if you like, it is the philosophy of balance. What am I to do in a world like this, when I never know what is going to meet me round the corner? I set out in the morning, what is going to happen? I do not know – anything may happen. Life is full of surprises, they come suddenly round the corners: 'none can know sincere felicity'. What am I to do? 'Keep an even mind,' says the Stoic. 'With equal mind, what happens, let us bear.' That is all you can do – bear it!

But how do you bear it? Here is his answer, and his prescription: 'Nor joy nor grieve too much for things beyond our care'. 'If you want to go through life standing on your feet,' says the Stoic, 'never be too happy, never be too joyful, because you never know what sorrow is coming to meet you. Do not let yourself go, never let yourself go, absolutely, in joy. Is not this the whole trouble today that people, in their youth especially, often give themselves over to unrelieved joy. Do not do it,' says the Stoic, 'you will be hurt by life. You must be careful.

'But on the other hand,' he adds, 'do not be too unhappy: "Nor joy nor grieve too much". If you want to go through life successfully,' says the Stoic, 'you must control your feelings and your emotions. You must hold them well in check and keep the rein tightly in your hands. You may be tempted to let yourself go in joy – don't do it! Hold back! Then grief comes; do not be extreme in your grief, hold it back too. Things are never as bad as they appear to be. Time is a great healer.' This is the philosophy of Stoicism – just hold on, stick it, do not be too happy, do not be too sorrowful. 'Nor joy nor grieve too much for things beyond our care.'

And then the final bit of philosophy: 'Like pilgrims to the appointed place we tend'. It is so true, is it not? What is the appointed place? For the Stoic, the world is an inn, it is like a hostelry in which he spends a night, and in the morning he pays his bill and on he goes. 'The world's an inn and death the journey's end.'

That, then, is typical Stoicism for you and it is the creed and belief of the vast majority of people in this country today. They have abandoned Christianity and that is how they are living. 'Anyhow', they say, 'we cannot do much about it.' There is an element of fatalism in it you see – you never know what is going to happen. What, then, do you do? Well, you keep yourself in control, education helps you to do so, and you use courage and you have your stiff upper lip. You will never be too happy, you are never too sorry. You simply go on, and thus you will just manage to keep on your feet; with your philosophy of balance, you maintain an even keel, and you will arrive at the journey's end. That is death and there is nothing beyond it. So you will just get through as best you can. That is life! But that is also hopelessness. That is Stoicism, my friend – negative! There is no joy, no happiness, no triumph. It is just refusing to fall. It is not going on triumphantly and glorying.

Now, let me put to you the Christian position in the form of another poem. But let me first tell you the story of the man who wrote it. He was a Christian who lived in Chicago in the United States in the last century and his name was H. G. Spafford. He was an attorney, a married man with four daughters and he was, moreover, a very successful man who had become wealthy. One summer, it was decided that Mrs Spafford and the girls should pay a visit to Europe to go round the various countries visiting the great cities and the great art treasures and so on. When the time came, Mr Spafford went down to the seaport with his wife and daughters and saw them on board the ship, and there he stood on the quayside waving to them as the ship set out for her voyage across the Atlantic. But, alas, in mid-Atlantic that ship collided with another and sank in a few minutes. The four daughters were drowned while Mrs Spafford, as by a miracle, was eventually picked up by a French boat and ultimately landed in France. From there she sent a cable to her husband saying, 'All lost! I alone remain. What shall I do?'

But that was not all. After the departure of Mrs Spafford and the girls, there had been a sudden bank crash – something which happened quite frequently in the last century. And in this bank crash in Chicago, Mr Spafford had lost all his wealth. In one afternoon, from being a very wealthy man he became a very poor one. So here was this Christian man who, having lost all his wealth and possessions, suddenly got a cable to say that his four darling daughters had been drowned in mid-Atlantic. How did he react to this? Did he say, 'I must not whimper, I must still carry on somehow, I must not give up. I must call upon all my reserves of courage, I must be a man, and I must not falter or fail?' No, no! That is Stoicism and this man was a Christian. This is how he reacted: he sat down and he wrote these words:

When peace like a river attendeth my way,
When sorrows like sea billows roll,
Whatever my lot, though hast taught me to say,
It is well, it is well, with my soul!

Do you see the difference? 'When peace like a river attendeth my way' – yes, and 'When sorrows like sea billows roll' – and rob me of my four, darling daughters in a second; 'Whatever my lot' – whether peace or sorrow – 'thou hast taught me to say, It is well, it is well, with my soul!' He is exulting! He is rejoicing! He is not merely negatively standing up and re-signing himself to his fate and deciding to go on somehow. No! 'It is well . . . !' 'Nevertheless I am not ashamed: for I know whom I have believed, and am persuaded that he is able to keep that which I have committed unto him against that day.'

You do not explain the apostle Paul in terms of tempera-ment, nor in terms of Stoic philosophy, nor in any other human explanations you may like to offer, because there is only one explanation for that which enables a man to speak like this. There is only one answer – it is his faith based upon his belief in the gospel of our Lord and Saviour Jesus Christ. It is that – and it is nothing else.

This, therefore, is the vital point and it is the one point, of course, that is made in the entire context. Now I am just introducing this subject at this point and I hope to go on to analyse it further. But I must make this introduction because if we are not right at this point we are going to be wrong everywhere. This I say is the vital point: it is the belief in the gospel alone that enables a man to overcome in this way and manner.

That raises for us the vital question as to what this gospel is – and this is, perhaps, the point at which there is the greatest confusion at this hour. So I want to put down certain general principles for your consideration. The first thing, evidently, that we are taught by the apostle is that the gospel is a complete view of life which covers all conceivable eventualities. The gospel, in other words, is not merely a matter of ethics and conduct and morality and behaviour. There are so many people who think it is. They still think that the Christian is just a man who lives a good life and who does not do certain things and who tries to do others. That is their whole conception of Christianity.

In the name of God I protest against such an attitude! This man, Paul, alone is enough to prove that that is wrong. This is a whole view of life. I have known many moral people who have been very miserable and who have had nothing that would sustain them when they were face to face with death and the end. Christianity is not just a question of political or social reform. Let me say it once more – it is not a mere protest against bombs or indulging in politics. That is not Christianity. Christianity is this total view that enables me to view life and death and all things, and to do so triumphantly. It is a total view. It is not merely some narrow, cramped, confined little system. It is that which enables a man to be exultant even in the midst of the storm.

But let me give you a second principle. The gospel, the Christian message, is not merely a vague message of comfort and of cheer; it does not merely help us by helping us to forget our troubles and our problems. There are many people who think of it like that. How often have we heard them say in this present century that Christianity is 'the dope of the masses', 'the opiate of the people'; that some people take Christianity as others take whisky and others take drugs, anything to help them to forget their troubles; and they think of us as people who meet in places of worship, who shut out the world and pull down the blinds, and sing our hymns and work ourselves up into an ecstasy and so feel very happy. They think we are happy just because we have been drugging ourselves; they believe we have stopped thinking, we have just indulged in a riot of the imagination. We have turned our backs upon life, they say, and upon all its attendant problems and circumstances.

But what a travesty! What a lie! Christianity is realistic. There is no more realistic book in the whole world today than the Bible. You see, that is where the Bible shocks all sorts of people. Some people think it is too good, and others that it is too bad. 'You have got all that stuff in the Old Testament,' they say, 'about David and his adultery and so on; it is not fit to put into the hands of nice young people.' But thank God for an honest book. Here it is, in the words of Cromwell, 'warts and all'. It is a realistic book, a frank book, and an honest one. The idea that Christianity is something that asks us to turn our backs upon life and its problems is quite wrong. This, and this alone, really asks us to face life and to face all the facts, and to face them at their worst. That is why I am stressing that it is a complete view.

You may tell me that your philosophy of life is enabling you to live, but I ask you what you mean by living. It may give you pleasure, but does it give you peace? Does it give your soul satisfaction? Does it give you comfort when you need it most of all? Is it really independent of your circumstances? Will it go on if your circumstances suddenly completely change? These are the tests. Does it cover death, because death is coming. Listen to the Stoic: '. . . death the journey's end'; 'every man who lives is born to die'. Does your philosophy cater for that? Can you die triumphantly? Or do you just turn your face to the wall and say, 'It is the end! It is all up, I've got to go' – no more? That is not triumph, that is not understanding. My dear friend, if you claim that your philosophy is adequate, well then it must cover all the facts and all the possibilities, and the Christian message does exactly that. The Christian message is not just a message that offers good cheer and comfort indiscriminately. It is not some sort of soporific. There is a harshness about it, a manliness, and an honesty. It tells you to deny yourself, to take up a cross and to follow Christ. This is not an easy life. 'For unto you it is given in the behalf of Christ, not only to believe on him, but also to suffer for his sake', says the apostle Paul to the Philippians. We read of him in Acts 14:22 telling the churches that 'through much tribulation [we must] enter into the kingdom of God'. This idea that Christianity says 'Believe in this and you will never have another problem' is an utter travesty. It is not true. Our Lord himself said at the end of his life, 'In the world ye shall have tribulation: but be of good cheer; I have overcome the world.' You see it is always the same thing. It does not turn its back upon the facts, it does not make you happy by ignoring them or by neglecting them. It overcomes them. It looks at them steadily and then it overcomes them, takes you through them, beyond them, triumphant and glorying, filled with joy and praise and thanksgiving.

And then I take you to a third principle which is this, shown here very plainly. The Christian message is not something that acts automatically without our doing anything at all about it. There are people who think of it like that and I am afraid there are some people who even try to use it in that way. But Christianity does not work like that; it does not work automatically, but by making us think, by making us apply the message. You see that was the whole trouble with Timothy. What the apostle is really saying to him, in effect, is this: 'Timothy, why are you forgetting the things I told you, why are you not applying the message that you have heard from me, why do you allow yourself to go down like that? If only you had reminded yourself of these things. You must stir up the gift that is in you.' It does not act automatically. And this again is a most important point at this present time. We must not think of Christianity as some sort of drug that has its inevitable effect upon us. Christianity is a truth that comes first and foremost to the mind; it addresses the understanding and, on the basis of that, it enables us to speak and to live as Paul does. It is not an automatic action.

And that brings me to my last fundamental principle which is that the Christian message, the Christian faith, has no comfort or consolation to offer us at all apart from our belief in its truth. Now this is the key principle. Christianity does not give us comfort directly; comfort is an indirect product, and the same is true of consolation and courage.

This, again, is where so many go astray. People get into trouble, something goes wrong in their lives; they are taken ill, lose their job, lose a husband or a wife, perhaps, and they suddenly find themselves bereft, all they had lived for has suddenly gone. They thought that they were quite happy, and they thought they had a philosophy of life, but they now discover that the foundation has gone, that there is nothing left. They do not know what to do and so they try the cults and various other things. And then they wonder whether the Christian Church can help them – they want comfort and they want it directly. But they will not get it. Christianity never gives direct comfort. You will never know the comfort and the consolation of the scriptures and of the gospel until you believe the gospel. You cannot have Christian comfort until you have become a Christian. That is the trouble – people are trying to get the benefits of Christianity without becoming Christians. It cannot be done. The benefits are the by-products. The thing that is essential is a belief in the faith.

Now, the apostle puts this very clearly before us: 'For the which cause I also suffer these things: nevertheless I am not ashamed'. Why not? 'For' – because – he can give a reason. I am not ashamed, I am not overwhelmed, I am not sinking, I am not giving up in despair, I am not frantic, I am not lost. Why? Well I will tell you. 'For I know whom I have believed, and am persuaded that he . . .' In other words, he deduces his comfort and his consolation from his faith and from his belief; and this is the most vital point of all.

Now you begin to see why the apostle handles this whole subject in the way that he does in this paragraph that we are looking at together. Why does he not merely write to Timothy and say, 'Timothy, you know, as a Christian you have no right to be like that, why don't you pull yourself together, man? Cheer up!' and leave it at that. He knows that that is not going to be any good at all. There is only one way whereby Timothy can be put right and that is by reminding him of the whole of the gospel. He has got to come back to the centre of the faith, then everything will be right. But not until then. There is no comfort, no consolation to be offered apart from the truth itself. Comfort, consolation and all other blessings are *derived* from the truth and are never to be obtained apart from it. It may sound harsh to you, but I must say it as I value your soul. You may be turning to Christianity because you want comfort, but the first question I must ask you is this: Are you a Christian? For if you are not a Christian I have no comfort to give you. You will never know comfort until you become a Christian. Your need is not comfort, it is a need of the knowledge of God and the knowledge of Christ. You must start at the centre. The gospel gives its blessings in its own way and there are no short cuts.

These, then, are the things that the great apostle emphasised here as he wrote to his young disciple and friend Timothy. Timothy was in trouble because he had forgotten these things or because he was not applying them as he should, because he was looking at circumstances instead of looking at the truth or at the circumstances in the light of the truth. And that, I say, is the main trouble with so many people at this present hour. There are people who come to us and say – 'Yes, I have tried your Christianity but it did not work with me, it did not give me the blessing that I wanted.' And they tell us the whole truth about themselves as they utter the very words. You see, they wanted this particular blessing but they have not got it. Of course not! Why? Because they are putting the blessing before Christ, before God, before the soul! And there are many today who say that Christianity is failing, and they say that because they know nothing about it. The foolish people who say – 'But look at the wars, look at the international situation! Your Christianity has been going for two thousand years and yet look at the state of the world, look at the terrible possibilities even now.' But Christianity never said that it was in the world to banish war, it never claimed to do so, it has never offered itself as a social or a political movement for reformation. That is not what it is for. It makes Christians, and until you get Christians, you will never get Christian experience, you will never get Christian living, you will never get Christian anything. You cannot get the by-products of Christianity unless you have a belief in the

Christian message first. So this is the first step that we must be clear about. We must know exactly what the Christian message is, and that is the point of the greatest confusion at this hour.

Let me, in conclusion, just give you some headings which I hope to work out in greater detail later on. What is this Christianity? I say there is no more vital question confronting anybody in the world today than just that. Here is the only thing that can give us hope, here is the only thing that can make us triumph in spite of life and its problems. So the vital question is – what is it? Here are some headings for you.

Christianity is something that can be defined. It is something specific, not something vague and nebulous. It is something that can be stated, and must be stated, in propositions. Now here, you see, we come to the very heart of the modern confusion. We are forever reading in the papers about this new theology and this new morality and so on and how it is no use coming to the twentieth century man with this old gospel. Modern man, we are told, thinks in new terms, he is a scientific man and so on, and he must have a new gospel, and the idea is that the gospel is something that cannot be defined. Christianity, we are told, is just some vague spirit. There was a slogan a few years ago that put it like this: 'Christianity is caught not taught.' In other words, you do not know what it is, but suddenly you find yourself taken up by this thing, you 'catch a spirit'. You do not know what has caught you nor what you have caught, but you feel differently and you want to do this, that and the other.

Or, as it is put at the present time, Christianity is nothing but love and goodness. So if you want to find it you do not go to a place of worship, you do not listen to preaching, you do not read the Bible, you go and mix with the common people, and there, as you mix with them, you will find a great deal of kindness, a great deal of love and a great deal of goodness, and that is God. That is God! That is Christian! You see, they tell us that we can be Christians without knowing it. It does not matter what a man believes; as long as he has this idea of goodness in him and wants to do good, he is a Christian, though he knows nothing – nothing about it at all.

I remember a very distinguished man writing an article some years ago and in it he said: 'My father was the greatest Christian that I have ever known, but, of course, he did not believe any of the doctrines of the Christian faith.' Now that is the common idea, is it not – that Christianity is something that cannot be defined and that indeed to attempt to define it is ridiculous and almost insulting; that the Church has spent her time with these definitions and so on, and has confused the people. 'We are not interested in doctrines,' they say, 'We are interested in life.' But, my dear friend, the whole argument of the apostle here is this, that you will never have the life without the doctrine – never! It is impossible. And he goes out of his way to show us that Christianity is not something vague and nebulous and indefinite, some wonderful spirit that you cannot understand.

What, then, is it? Well, notice the terms Paul uses. He says, in talking here about the gospel: 'Whereunto I am appointed a preacher, and an apostle, and a teacher.' Well, a teacher, by definition, is a man who has got something to teach. A teacher does not teach nothing, he is not just an exhorter. A teacher is not just a man who stands up and says 'I am very happy and I would like you all to be happy as well, and if you only go out into life you will find happiness.' No! 'A *teacher*'! A teacher has got a subject, he has material.

But the apostle does not leave it even at that. Listen to the further terms that he uses. 'Hold fast', he says to Timothy, 'the form of sound words, which thou hast heard of me, in faith and love which is in Christ Jesus.' There is a 'form' of sound words. Now the Greek word, here translated form, is a most interesting word. It means a pattern, or a model, or if you like, a sort of preliminary sketch with which the artist starts, and on which he builds up his picture. That is the very word which the apostle uses. He says, 'Timothy, you know your whole trouble is that you are not holding fast this body of doctrine that you have heard from me – this form, this content, these declarations, these propositions of the faith.' That body of doctrine is the very thing the apostle is exhorting Timothy to lay hold on. And then he uses still another word in verse fourteen: 'That good thing' – which we should translate: 'that good deposit' – 'which was committed unto thee, keep by the Holy Ghost which dwelleth in us.'

So you see, according to the apostle Paul, Christianity is far from being some vague wonderful spirit of love and peace which a man enjoys though he knows not how he has got it nor how he can give it to others. It is quite the reverse. It is a body of doctrine, it is a number of statements, it is a particular teaching, it is something that you can tell people and can put to them in propositions.

Paul puts it like that positively, but then, notice the way in which he puts it negatively. 'Hold fast', he says, 'the form of *sound* words.' All words are not sound; some words are wrong. There were false teachers even in the days of the early Church in the first century, and the apostle says, 'I am not asking you to hold fast every word, hold fast the form of sound words, healthy words, good words, right words. Not only can I state Christianity in propositions, not only can I say "It is this"; I can equally say, "It is not that"!' Christianity is to be defined, and it is to be contrasted with error and with heresy. Of course all this is dismissed today and people ridicule it. They say, 'What does it matter whether a man believes in God or not, he is going to be in heaven. We shall see atheists in heaven, what does it matter whether a man believes in the resurrection or not? What does it matter whether a man believes in the atoning death of Christ? What does it matter whether he believes in miracles? Nothing matters except that he is a good man.' But according to this great apostle and according to the whole of the Bible, if a man does not believe these things he is not a Christian and he will never know the benefits of Christianity.

And thirdly, he uses this great word 'Guard'! Hold it fast! Protect it! Defend it! Argue round it! Do not let them take it from you! 'Stand fast in the faith'! This is the truth, do not let anybody detract from it, let nobody subtract from it in any sense whatsoever. Now there is the typical statement of the apostle and he puts it still more specifically in the next chapter in verse eight. 'Remember', he says, 'that Jesus Christ of the seed of David was raised from the dead according to my gospel.' *My* gospel! There are other people preaching other gospels but they are not *the* gospel. They are liars! They are cheats! They are self-appointed! Do not listen to them. My gospel! The Christian truth is a truth that can be defined, that can be stated in propositions. We must know what they are and we must believe them. God willing I am going to try to proceed to tell you what these absolute essentials of the Christian faith are. They are all in this paragraph. The apostle reminds Timothy of every one of them. That is the first thing.

Here is the second: it is based on authority – the authority of the apostles. 'That good thing', he says, '. . . which ye have heard of me,' hold on to it, pass it on.

And thirdly: Christianity is based upon historical events and facts. Paul says, it 'is now made manifest by the appearing . . .' It is not a philosophy, it is based upon facts, and is changeless – and that of necessity, because it is based upon facts. But thank God that while the Christian faith is changeless, it is something that changes us, and changes our whole outlook and our entire life; it gives us a new view of time, a new view of eternity, a new view of everything. And above all it gives us power. 'Be not thou therefore ashamed of the testimony of our Lord, nor of me his prisoner: but be thou partaker of the afflictions of the gospel according to the power of God.' It does not leave it to us. Believing the truth we receive a power that enables us to say, 'For the which cause I also suffer these things: nevertheless I am not ashamed: for I know whom I have believed, and am persuaded that he is able to keep that which I have committed unto him' – my soul and its safe keeping – 'against that day.'

We have only introduced this great theme so far, but I do trust that you will keep this thought uppermost in your mind: that no man ever can know the comfort and the consolation and the power of the Christian faith until he knows what that faith is and until he has believed it. So the first great question is – what is this faith? What is this truth? What is this message that I must believe, that will change me and make me see everything else in a different way and give me power that will make me more than conqueror over everything that is set against me?

It is Jesus Christ, and him crucified! It is God so loving the world, that he sent his only begotten son, that whosoever believeth in him should not perish, but have everlasting life. It is the message that tells you how you can be reconciled to God and then begin to receive those blessings that God alone can give you.

I hope to work these things out in greater detail as we go on. But here is the beginning of it all: 'Believe on the Lord Jesus Christ, and thou shalt be saved.'

Chapter Two

SUNDAY EVENING SERMON
April 19th 1964

Real Christianity

For the which cause I also suffer these things: nevertheless I am not ashamed: for I know whom I have believed, and am persuaded that he is able to keep that which I have committed unto him against that day (2 Tim. 1:12).

As we have seen, the context of this glowing and glorious statement is very important. The apostle is writing to Timothy, a young minister, one of his own disciples, who was obviously an apprehensive kind of individual and one who was ready to lose hope when there were difficulties to be faced. Read again the whole passage which surrounds the verse. In it Paul makes a tremendous asseveration. Here is a man in prison, a man weary in his great work of travelling and preaching the gospel, and now, as the result of the misunderstanding and the malignity of men, lying a helpless prisoner. Indeed, he is a prisoner of perhaps the most capricious of all the Roman emperors, the Emperor Nero, and liable to be put to death at any moment. There he is in the prison and yet this is how he writes. 'I am not ashamed' – I am not in any trouble, I am not disappointed, I am not losing hope, all is well with me – 'I am not ashamed: for I know whom I have believed, and am persuaded that he is able to keep that which I have committed unto him against that day.'

We are not, therefore, dealing with a bit of theory here, this is a man giving his experience. Christianity is the most practical thing in the world today. It is a way of life. It is something that offers men and women an experience, and here is an example of what it offers. It offers to make a man more than conqueror over everything that may be set against him, and when it says that, it includes everything. There is nothing omitted – more than conqueror in all things, prison, death, anything!

Here, then, is this tremendous statement of the apostle's experience, but of course it also comes as a challenge to us. What about us? How are we getting on in life? You see this is the essence of the Christian message. We do not go to church in order that we may tell the President of the United States, or the Russian leader or our own Prime Minister how they ought to run the country. We do not go there to discuss politics or similar subjects, we are there to discuss life and living. We are not theorists, we are realists and we are facing the battle and the problem of life. This is the test of all our talk, all our theorising: does it help us? Does it really work? I know it is the simplest thing in the world to get up in a debating society or to speak in private discussions and to lay down the law and say what we think. But the whole test is, what does it all lead to? Does it satisfy?

The apostle is here preaching to us a gospel that works. He was a living illustration and example of it. But what about us? We are driven to ask ourselves this obvious question, where do we stand? How do we find ourselves in life at this very moment? After all, the important thing for us is to discover what it is that makes this attitude to life possible. Would you not like to have that kind of experience which enables you to say with Paul what he says here or what he says elsewhere? Read him saying the same sort of thing to the Philippians: 'I have learned, in whatsoever state I am, therewith to be content. I know both how to be abased, and I know how to abound . . . I can do all things through Christ which strengtheneth me.' 'For me to live in Christ, and to die is gain.' These are his great assertions. Would not we all like to be like that? Would you not like to be a master of life? Would you not like to go through the world 'more than conqueror'? It is possible, says this man. How, then, is it possible?

We have already begun to consider that question. We have seen that it cannot be explained in terms of a man's natural temperament, his psychology, or whatever religious leanings he may have. The glory of this gospel is that it can do these things for a man whatever his temperament, and these other views are just disproved completely by the Bible and by the subsequent history of the Christian Church. In the Church today, as at all other times, you can find all the conceivable combinations and permutations of character, temperament, psychology – whatever you may like to call it. Thank God that this is the case! This is not a hope merely for certain kinds of people; it is offered as a hope to any and to all. 'Whosoever'! 'Whosoever comes' he can have this.

Neither, we saw, is Paul's strength to be explained in terms of the fact that he may have adopted the philosophy of Stoicism. We saw that there is a vital difference. Stoicism is always negative, it is resignation. There is never a note of triumph in Stoicism. It is 'grit', it is 'stick it', it is will-power, it is courage. It may be very noble, I will grant you that, but it is noble paganism. The Stoic does not know what it is to sing. Here is a man who is singing in a prison, he is more than conqueror. This is not Stoicism.

Now the apostle himself, you remember, tells us that there is only one explanation of this great assertion, and that is that he believes the gospel of our Lord and Saviour Jesus Christ. It is because he has preached the gospel that he is a prisoner, but he says all is well, because even though he is in prison yet the gospel enables him to sing here. And so, as I have said, there is nothing in the world that can really help us, face to face with the ultimate questions, but this gospel. It is vital, therefore, for us to know exactly what the gospel is. And, alas, it is just here that we find ourselves confronted by an appalling confusion.

Let me say this once more. I have great sympathy with the modern man, and with the masses of people who are outside the Christian Church today. It must be very difficult for them to know what the gospel is in view of some of the things they are having to listen to and some of the things they read. And that is why we are considering all this so carefully.

We have seen very clearly that the gospel is not just a message of comfort. The Church is not a dispensary giving out anodynes, it does not exist merely to dispense some soothing syrup. The gospel gives truth, and the comfort is the result of the truth. You cannot bypass the truth and merely get what you want. You may want physical healing, you may want this and that, guidance and all sorts of things; you cannot get them apart from the gospel. The gospel is to be believed first, then one of its products or by-products is the comfort and the ability to live that we so much desire.

So we return to this vital consideration – what is this gospel? – and here we face the modern difficulties. And, again, what I want to do at this point is purely introductory. I spend time like this on introductions because I know in my own life, and in my experience in handling others who are in difficulties, that we go wrong generally right at the beginning. People are always ready to argue about the implications of the gospel, when what they need to discuss is what the gospel actually is. And I find that most people go wrong with regard to the gospel in their very approach to it – at the very beginning – and that means that they must be wrong everywhere else.

What, then, are these difficulties? We have looked, first of all, at the teaching which says that one cannot define the gospel, that teaching and doctrine are unnecessary and that it is just something that gives one a good feeling. We have seen Paul's answer to that in this passage, how he enjoins Timothy to 'hold fast the form of sound words'. The gospel can be defined. The apostle defines it here and that is what we are going to consider together.

But, in order that I may further establish this fact, take the story that is found in Acts 17. There we see Paul in Athens. He walks around and sees the place cluttered with temples, and he tells the Athenians that they are 'too religious'. They have so many gods that there is hardly room for the temples in which they might worship them all. 'You are too superstitious', says Paul, 'you are too religious.'

Then he begins to reason and to debate with them. 'May we

know', the Athenians ask him, 'what this new doctrine, whereof thou speakest, is?' And Paul is not in the slightest difficulty. They appoint a time, and they meet together on Mars' Hill and he begins to tell them what this new doctrine is, and notice the term that he uses. 'I declare', he says, 'I declare unto you'.

The apostle was able to give an exposition of his doctrine. He did not merely tell them, 'Well, you know, I have had a wonderful experience, I have got a wonderful feeling within me now. I have found love. I find that when you really get to know people, you begin to forget yourself, and as you go out and mix with people and try to help them and understand them, you have a different view of them, you have a nice feeling within you. That is it – that is what I am preaching.' That is not what he said at all! He began to speak and preach specific doctrines about God the Creator and about Christ and about judgment, and so on. It is a teaching, it is a definite doctrine, it is a body of truth, it is a form of sound words. The Bible is full of that. And the early Church held on to this same point, as indeed has the Church throughout the ages.

I do not want to entertain you by criticising others; God forbid that I should do so. But there is something laughable about some of these modern teachers. They tell us in their books and sermons that you cannot define the doctrine, you cannot define Christianity, that you cannot state it in propositions, and in the very service in which they say that, at a given point they get the congregation to recite the Apostles' Creed, or some other confession of faith.

What are these creeds, or confessions? They are nothing but statements, propositions, definitions of proof. They say Christianity is that which asserts this: 'I believe; I believe; I believe', and we have our series of propositions. That is Christianity! That was the position of the early Church. I do not mean by that that the apostles actually drew up that creed; they did not. But it is called the Apostles' Creed quite rightly because it enshrines the very message that was preached by the apostles. It is a wonderful summary of their preaching. The fathers met together in the great councils in the early centuries of the Christian Church, because false teaching was coming in and, guided by the Holy Spirit, they laid down the truth in propositions. And, as Paul says here, you can draw a distinction between 'sound words' and words that are not sound. 'Hold fast', he says, 'the form of sound [healthy] words, which thou hast heard of me.' Listen, he says, to me, not to the false teachers. 'My gospel', he says in the next chapter, and the creeds and the confessions summarise or repeat what we find laid down so clearly here by the great apostle and, indeed, what is laid down everywhere in the New Testament.

Now let us be clear about this: you *can* know what Christianity is. It is not a vague feeling, it is not something nebulous. It is something that can be described and defined and stated in propositions. You can know whether you believe it or whether you do not. The apostle's preaching at Athens divided the congregation into two groups; those who did not believe and those who did. It has always done that and it is still doing so.

The second difficulty is that there are people who do not have the experience of the apostle Paul because they do not believe the gospel, and they do not believe it because they think it has failed. How often do we hear today that the gospel has failed? Perhaps you have said so yourself. We have all said it at some time or other in our ignorance. 'What is the use', people say, 'of preaching Christianity to us? Christianity has been in this world now for nearly two thousand years yet look at the state of the world. If your gospel were true the world would not be as it is. Your gospel has failed.'

This is a most interesting position, but when I am presented with it, I always ask this question: 'What does the gospel promise? If you say it has failed, what do you think the gospel has promised to do?' That is surely the question to ask, is it not? If you tell me that the gospel of Jesus Christ has failed, then it is obvious to me that you must have some idea in your mind as to what the gospel has offered to do. What is this? And the moment I ask that question, the reply will be something like this: 'The gospel has promised to put an end to war, to banish poverty and suffering, to reform the world, to undo wrongs, to mitigate injustices and to make a better world. That is what the gospel has offered and promised to do, but it has not done it, and the modern world is proof enough that it has not.'

Now, there is only one simple answer to that. The gospel has never promised to do such things – never! There is not a scintilla of evidence that can be produced to show that the gospel has offered and promised to put an end to war. Our Lord at the very end of his life said, 'And ye shall hear of wars and rumours of wars' (Matt. 24:6). He also said, 'But as the days of Noah were, so shall also the coming of the son of man be.' As it was in Sodom and Gomorrah, 'even thus shall it be in the day when the son of man is revealed.' He has never promised to banish war, or to reform the world. There is no evidence whatsoever. It is people who import this into the gospel, this is what they think it is. People have got these utterly erroneous ideas, and because Christianity does not do what they think it has promised to do they dismiss it and do not experience its benefits. But the trouble is they have never known what Christianity is, and they have never understood the gospel. The second difficulty, you see, drives us back to the same position: we must discover what Christianity is.

We now move on to the next difficulty – and I am simply picking out the commonest problems that people seem to have. The third is that people say, 'It is monstrous to ask a man in the twentieth century to consider a gospel that was preached in the first century. It really is about time you Christians woke up and realised that we are not in the world as it used to be. We, after all, are twentieth-century people, you know, we are living in the atomic age. My dear man,' they continue, 'you are living not only pre-war, you are almost primitive. Where are you, where do you live; don't you know that things have happened and things are moving, and that we have got all this great scientific knowledge; the modern man is an entirely different man from what man used to be, and his problems are all together different? What is the use of asking us to consider some old message like this?'

Now, there are two fallacies there. The first one is the belief that man is different. Are the problems of man essentially different today from what they have always been? Surely I need not tell you what these problems are? They are not the splitting of the atom, not the sending of a man up into outer space – those are not the problems. The problems are: what is life; how can a man live in a decent manner; how can a man control himself and his impatience and his basér instincts and desires; how can a man live as a man; how can he so live that even if he is stricken down by an illness, or shattered by an accident and loses everything on which he has depended, he is still all right; how can a man sing in a prison? These are the questions. How can a man die? They have always been the questions, they are still the same; there are no new problems. And the greatest of them all, I say, is this ultimate problem of, what is man? Is he supreme, or is there someone beyond him? And is it, as the Bible says, man's relationship to this someone who is beyond him that matters above everything else?

There, then, is the wrong assumption in this third difficulty. The problems have not changed. We get so excited, we talk about science and wonderful discoveries. We think we are in a different realm. We are not, you know! Man still eats, he still drinks, he has still got sex, and these are the biggest problems of all. The scientific problems are child's play compared with these. These are *the* problems. The scientists can handle the others well enough. They have conquered the force of gravity, but they still have not conquered the force of sin. No, let us begin to think, my friends. We talk too much, we get too excited about our magical scientific terms. The elemental problems remain unchanged, absolutely what they have always been. And of course, as I am going to show you, the gospel, being what it is, does not change either. So what it was in the first century it was also in the tenth century, and it is still iñ the twentieth century because of its own essential nature.

Those are the three main difficulties and they all point in the same direction. It is because men do not know what the gospel really is that they go wrong at almost every point. What *is* its message? What does it promise? What has it got to give? My claim for it – let me say it once more – is just this: that what the gospel offers, it does give. What it promises, it performs. This man Paul is a witness to it. The saints of the centuries are witnesses to it. Thank God some of us in spite of our imperfections are living witnesses of it today! This is not theory, this is fact. I would not be a preacher of the gospel if it did not work. This is no profession to me. I did not come into a pulpit because I want a profession. I am privileged to preach these things because they are not only true, they work – and they work because they are true. So it is no use proceeding to argue about details or to consider particular problems unless you are clear about this fundamental question – What is the gospel? Can it be known? I have already answered, it can. How, then, can we know it, how are we to approach it?

Let me put it like this. What is our authority? I ask this because there are, I know, probably some people who are saying to themselves at this point, 'Ah yes, here it comes, I thought it would be that. This fellow, of course, is conceited, he thinks that what he says is right, and that because he is saying it, it must be right. It is the typical dogmatism of the preacher.'

There are many answers to that. We are all dogmatic, are we not? When you say, 'This is what I say', you are being dogmatic. So you are condemning yourself. But I am not actually saying all this because it is what I think; that is not my position at all. I am simply a little expositor of this Word, and if you can prove to me that I am doing any violence to what the great apostle teaches, I will give in and admit that I am wrong. I am simply holding before you and expounding to you what this man of God tells us, and what men of God have said, as I have reminded you, throughout the running centuries.

What, then, is the authority? There are only two answers to that question. Ultimately, either we all trust to our reason, to our understanding, to our opinion and that of other people like ourselves, or else we accept the teaching of the Bible as the revelation of God. There are no other positions. It is one or the other. In the last analysis we either trust to what we think, what we understand, what we believe, or else we submit ourselves utterly and absolutely to this book. We say, 'I know nothing, speak to me, give it to me', and we come to it as little children. It is one or the other.

I must, therefore, hold these two before you. I do so because, as I said at the beginning, this is something that affects not only the whole of a man's life but also his death. This is the thing that changes everything, that enables a man to triumph in the worst conditions conceivable. This is what matters above all else; you either rely on your reason, or else you submit to the revelation. Now I am pleading with you to submit to the revelation, and I do so for several reasons.

Let me first of all show you the inadequacy of reason, the inadequacy of human wisdom, or, if you like, the total inadequacy of philosophy. For a hundred years now this has been the real fight – the fight between philosophy and revelation – and all the higher criticism of the Bible is based on human philosophy. Indeed the whole trouble with the Church of Rome is that it has added human philosophy to the Bible. It believes the Bible, yes, but it has so added human philosophy, derived from Aristotle, that this philosophy contradicts the teaching of the Bible. So I do not accept the authority of the Roman Church, I accept the authority of this book.

Let us look at it then. Why do I say that reason is inadequate? This is a great subject, of course, and I can simply suggest some headings. The great quest of man from the beginning, the great quest of civilisation, has been the quest and the search for wisdom. Job propounded the old question: 'Where is the place of wisdom?' Every thoughtful man always comes to that. The man who has any brains at all, and who uses them, has always thought and ruminated over life, and in the end he has said, 'Oh, where is the place of wisdom?' We are living in an age which does not give sufficient attention to it, which is only interested in cleverness. The true thinkers are interested not in cleverness, but in wisdom – that is what they all want to find.

Now, what wisdom seeks is an understanding of man. What

is man? Before you begin to ask what can be done for man or what does man need, you must ask that question. If you do not know what man is, how can you possibly cater for him? Is man an animal? If he is, treat him as such. That is being done today. But if man is not an animal but something more, then he needs something more. What is man? Wisdom has been trying to answer that question throughout the centuries. What is life? What is our life in this world, what is it meant to be, what are we meant to be doing? I say again, how can a man so live that he can go to bed happily at night and look at himself in the mirror without feeling ashamed, that he can put his head down on the pillow and sleep like a little child, as the psalmist did, though surrounded by his enemies. 'I laid me down and slept; I awaked; for the Lord sustained me.' Can we say this? That is the question. These are the things that wisdom has always been seeking for, the quiet mind, the quiet heart; the place of rest, the place of peace.

We have seen how the Stoics were grappling with these things, and how they arrived at their particular solution, which is not a solution. And then beyond all these, there are other great questions: how to die – what lies beyond? Wisdom has always been seeking to answer these questions, too. These have been the whole field of investigation for the philosophers of the centuries. But, philosophy has failed, it has always failed. It is still failing, and it does so because man is not pure reason. If we were pure reason, if we were just intellects, I suppose we would solve our problems. But we are not, and we know we are not.

What are we then? Well, the trouble with all of us is that there is an irrational element in us and it is even stronger than our reason. Though a man knows what is right he does wrong. He is irrational and contradictory. A man does something wrong and he says to himself, 'I will never do that again.' He is filled with shame and remorse, he is miserable, and he is honest. He says, 'I will never do it again.' But he does it again, and goes on repeating it. Irrationality! It is the essence of man's problems. There are forces in him that are stronger than his mind; there are drives; there are impulses; there are

intuitions. These are the things! The apostle Paul has summed
it up for us once and for ever: 'To will is present with me; but
how to perform that which is good I find not. For I delight in
the law of God after the inward man: but I see another law in
my members, warring against the law of my mind, and
bringing me into captivity to the law of sin which is in my
members' (Rom. 7:18,22,23). Man is a contradiction. The
irrational element is always there, and it foils all his Utopias
and upsets all his calculations.

But not only that. Reason is a very wonderful thing – I am
not here to say a word against it; in fact I am trying my best at
this moment to reason with you. I try to do it always. When I
preach, I do not tell stories about myself or anybody else, I do
not just make people sing choruses and try to work them
up – I reason with them. God forbid that I should say a word
against reason. I believe it is the gift of God to man, the thing
that differentiates him from an animal. But reason does not
help us at the most important points in life and with respect to
the most important things. Oh, most wonderful experiences
in life are really apart from reason; reason does not know
anything about love. The heart! The heart of man! 'The heart
hath its reasons', says one of the greatest reasoners that the
world has ever known – Blaise Pascal, that brilliant mathematician of the seventeenth century – 'The heart hath its
reasons which reason knows nothing of.' And how true it is.
Reason does not understand some of the most delicate human
relationships, or some of our most glorious experiences, and
reason cannot help us with them.

Let me sum up all this in order that I may move on. It has
been stated so perfectly by Robert Browning in his great
poem, 'Bishop Blougram's Apology'. The young man, full of
his philosophy and his ideas, comes and argues with the old
bishop. He has got everything tabulated, he has got it all
taped, as it were, by his reason, and the old bishop looks at
him, and he smiles at him and says, 'yes, I know exactly, I was
once like that myself, I thought I understood it all. But you
know,' he says, 'just when you have worked it all out and you
think you have got it all tabulated,

Just when we're safest, there's a sunset-touch,
A fancy from a flower-bell, some one's death,
A chorus-ending from Euripides,
And that's enough for fifty hopes and fears,
The grand perhaps.'

What is he talking about? Well, what he is saying is that just when you think you have understood it all through our perfect intellectual system, and you are, if you like in modern terminology, logical positivists and all is well, you suddenly see a sunset, and something happens within you that you cannot rationalise or explain; you are just moved. 'A fancy from a flower-bell'! Just a little flower in a hedgerow can do something to you that all our reason can neither do nor understand.

Or take the poet Wordsworth putting the same point in another way, when he says: 'To me the meanest flower that blows can give thoughts that do often lie too deep for tears', again something you cannot reason, you cannot rationalise, you cannot explain. But these are the things that elevate, that make life life, and that make a man a man. 'A fancy from a flower-bell, some one's death.' Some one suddenly taken! And you had got your perfect plan of life, you had not realised that it really was not kept going by our great intellectual system, but by this other one whom we loved and who meant more than life to you; and they are taken and you are left alone, and our whole system collapses. 'Some one's death'! Or perhaps, 'A chorus-ending from Euripides'. Some great piece of literature or a great piece of music. You cannot analyse it, we cannot explain it, but it has done something to you, it has lifted you up and you are in a realm where reason cannot penetrate. 'The heart hath its reasons which reason knows nothing of.'

And then, to add to all that there is this sense of the unseen that is in us, every one of us, the sense of powers round and about us greater than ourselves – hence paganism. That is what Paul found in Athens. Now do not forget that Athens was Athens! It was the Mecca of all the philosophers; it was the great seat of learning. And yet the thing that struck the apostle in this greatest intellectual city in the world was that it was full of temples. Why? There is only one explanation: their philosophy could not take them far enough. Philosophy was all right as far as it went, but they began to feel there were certain intangible elements that they could not understand. 'There are', they said, 'other forces working upon us that we do not know: there are gods – the god of peace, the god of love, the god of war!' And they erected temples to them, they tried to please and to placate them, these other unseen forces and powers. And especially that One they could not arrive at. They had a feeling that behind all appearances there was some great being controlling all. They called him The Un-known God! They could not discover the truth about him, try as they would. 'The world by wisdom', as Paul puts it to the Corinthians, 'knew not God'. They tried their utmost, but they could not arrive, because he ever eluded them. The mind was inadequate, the reason was not sufficient. That is why philosophy fails. It can only bring you to the point where you feel there is an Unknown God, there is a factor that we cannot define, that we cannot discover.

Why cannot man find God? Why is reason inadequate? The answer to these questions is a double one. In the first place it is because God is who and what he is, because of his greatness and his glory. 'No man hath seen God at any time.' The Lord said, 'There shall no man see me, and live'.

> Immortal, invisible, God only wise
> In light inaccessible hid from our eyes,
> Most blessed, most glorious, the ancient of days,
> Pavilioned in splendour, and girded with praise.

'God is light, and in him is no darkness at all.' What is the use of talking about the mind of man, what is the use of talking about reason, what is the value of our analyses, what is the value of all our scientific knowledge? It is useless!

And the modern world is confessing this. As the ancient world with all its philosophy and learning had to turn to the gods for the ultimate explanation, so with all our modern sophisticated education, for with all our knowledge and learning, we find in the Sunday papers . . . The astrologist! Fate! These other unseen powers! It is all because man by definition cannot arrive at a knowledge of God. 'Our God is a consuming fire' and man is not only finite he is fallen, he is sinful, and, as I say, he is irrational, even his brain has fallen. He is sinful, he is unworthy, he lacks spirituality, and God is spirit. The whole realm is different, and man is therefore totally inadequate. The best to which reason can bring him is a belief in force, in power, or in some influence. But that is not a knowledge of God. Reason ought to bring us to that. Paul argues in Romans 1 that man is inexcusable, that God has left his marks. You ought to look at a flower and see God. No man can explain that. That has not merely happened! – the perfection, the form, the arrangement. That is God! God the creator! His wisdom, his power, his creatorship.

Oh, how little we know! How little we know in theory. A symposium has been published by a number of scientific humanists and one of them has admitted very candidly that they all disagree about everything except about scientific facts. They do not agree about morals, for example. They all have great brains, they are very able men, and yet they disagree about everything except about sheer scientific facts. And here is my simple argument. If these great brains cannot arrive at certitude and at knowledge, where do the rest of us come in? What is the hope for mankind today, for the teeming masses in this world? We are not all great brains, we are not all great philosophers, we have not all had the advantage of an education at a university. But here are men who have, and they do not know! They disagree – every man has his own pet theory and idea – and if they cannot agree, what about us? What hope is there for us? There is none! If salvation depends upon man's reason and understanding, there is no hope, especially for the majority of us; but there is actually no hope for any.

It is because of this that we have the Bible. This is God's answer to them. It was when the world by wisdom knew not God, 'it pleased God through the foolishness of the thing preached to save them that believe'. God gave the world a great opportunity to arrive at knowledge, to arrive at truth, to arrive at perfection, to arrive at a true way of living, but it failed, and failed completely. The immorality and the vice of the Roman Empire at the end of the first century before Christ, and in the time of Christ and after, was appalling. The world today is rapidly going back to that, in spite of the flowering period of Greek philosophy. And then God sent the way of salvation, this thing that Paul declared to that learned congregation in Athens, and that he summarises here in writing to his disciple Timothy. Here is the truth, and here is the authority.

'Why believe that?' says someone. Well, I will tell you. This is entirely different. The Bible is based upon what it calls 'revelation'. There is not a single writer in the Bible who tells us, 'Now look here, listen to me, I have been grappling with this problem for many years and I have considered the different theories and I have at last come to this conclusion. I commend it to you, listen to this.' Not one! What they say is this: 'The word of the Lord came unto me.' Look at Paul, why does he preach this gospel? Is it that he has worked it out? Read his story and you will find that it is the exact opposite. He was a man who hated Christ, hated his gospel, hated the Church, thought he was doing God service by persecuting the Church, and yet now here he is preaching the gospel and rejoicing in it. How did he ever come to this? Oh, there is only one answer – revelation! He saw the Lord of glory on the road to Damascus and he was given the message – and he is always careful to say that. 'I delivered unto you', he says, 'first of all that which I also received.' It is not his theory. None of the Biblical writers claim it as their theory, they have been given the message. This message is a word from God! It is not a text-book of philosophy, not an aggregate of ideas; all this claims to be from God. Not man but God, giving! The message is given.

And, of course, as you read it, you begin to understand what it is talking about. You find a majesty here and a glory and a nobility in the message which you will never find anywhere else. You find a transcendent truth about God not only beyond man's reason but beyond his imagination. No man, no poet at the height of his inspiration has ever come anywhere near it. It must be a revelation from God. The very nature of the truth confirms what the Bible claims.

And then you think of its ennobling and elevating character, of how you feel when you read it – truly as if you had a spiritual bath – how you are searched and examined and made to feel ashamed; and how good and noble desires are stimulated within you, and a longing after a better life. Then you notice the unity of its message – sixty-six books written at different times by different people from different backgrounds, and yet one great central unified theme from Genesis to Revelation, all about a certain person. The unity of the book is clear in spite of all these differences.

And then there is the notable fact of prophecy, and this is a most amazing argument – how especially amazing that about eight hundred years before the birth of Jesus of Nazareth, most of the main facts in connection with him were already predicted and prophesied. You find them in the prophecy of Isaiah, and the other prophecies – even Bethlehem is mentioned. All the details about his being sold for thirty pieces of silver, about his riding on an ass, his death, his resurrection, they are all there. Prophecy! Fulfilled in detail! You have got to explain this, my friend. These are proofs that it is revelation.

And another thing I want to emphasise is that the Bible is history. This is not a book of theory but a book of history, a book of action. That is why you get so much about kings and princes and wars and marriages and deaths. History! The history of the Jews – things that happened to them. And above all it is about the history of this one central person, Jesus of Nazareth, the one who came, lived and died, rose from the dead and ascended. Here are facts! Paul preached 'Jesus and the resurrection'. He was preaching history, he was preaching facts, and the doctrines that come out of the facts, their significance and meaning. These are the things I want to unfold to you, God willing, but I am reminding you now of this general position. That is why we believe this, it is history, and it is what God has done, what he has revealed concerning his purposes.

And what do you and I really know apart from this? You see this is the thing that we must come to; when everything else fails, we turn to this. Now, people may say to me at this point, 'That sounds all right, but is that still the authority in this twentieth century?' Well can you not see, in the light of what I have just been saying, that time obviously does not enter into the thing at all? If this is a revelation from the everlasting and eternal God, what has time got to do with it? Has God changed? Do the changing scenes of time affect God? Does the fact that man has split the atom and conquered the force of gravity make any difference to God? The answer is no! And this is not man and his wisdom and knowledge groping and trying to arrive. It is God! The unchanging God revealing the truth concerning himself and man, and all his purposes. So that time makes no difference. What God revealed about himself in the first century is as true today as it was then, and what he had revealed before that is still true. God is still the same God. He cannot change. He is 'the Father of lights, with whom is no variableness, neither shadow of turning'. He is the everlasting God – Jehovah! I am! From eternity to eternity, who always was, always is, always will be. So that time, I say again has nothing to do with it. And as I have shown you, man does not change either, and the great questions remain. Man! Life! Living! Death! What lies beyond death! These are the questions, and what do we know about them? We know nothing. Nothing at all! And yet man will not believe this; he says 'I know'! But he does not know.

So, then, we come to this. We either go on muddling as we are in uncertainty, failing at every point and facing the unknown with nothing to guide us; or else we submit to God's revelation. And we submit to the whole of this. You and I are not in a position to pick and choose. We cannot say 'I believe this bit and I do not believe that.' Why not? Because we do not know anything, so we are not in a position to judge, and we cannot estimate. It is no use our saying 'I believe God is love, but I do not believe in his wrath.' How do we know, we know nothing about God. We would not know that he was love were it not that we are told it. But the book that tells us that God is love also tells us that God hates sin and is going to punish it. We either take it all or we reject it all. We cannot bring our minds in at certain points, and reason here and there. That is what people are doing today, and there is no gospel left and the churches arc being emptied. I am not surprised. And hell is being let loose, and it will get worse.

There is only one thing to do and that is to admit our utter ignorance, to be honest enough to confess that all our ideas are pure speculation, that we cannot prove anything; we must admit that it is simply that we say it and that we think it. And we contradict one another and we often contradict even ourselves. My dear man, my dear woman, there is only one thing to do. If you want to live a life that will make you more than conqueror, if you want to be able to sing in prison, if you want to have the joy which is possible even in the midst of tribulations, there is only one thing for you to do, and that is to submit yourself to this, to become, as Christ said, 'as a little child'. He said, 'Except ye be converted, and become as little children, ye shall not enter into the kingdom of heaven.' He said to Nicodemus, a very wise and able man, 'Verily, verily, I say unto thee, except a man be born again, he cannot see the kingdom of God.' It is as though he said, 'It is no use, you cannot go from where you are to where I am, you must be born again, you need to be re-made from the very foundation. You have got to start anew.' We have got to do what this man Paul did on the road to Damascus. He set out on his journey that day 'breathing out threatenings and slaughter' against the Christian Church; he hated Christ and all about him. Then he saw him, and in utter helplessness he said, 'Lord, what wilt thou have me to do?' He made a complete surrender! He believed, he accepted the message and that is the thing that accounts for what we read of in this very passage.

Here is the message: 'God so loved the world, that he gave his only begotten son,' even to the death on the cross; 'so that whosoever believeth in him should not perish but have everlasting life. Our greatest need is to know God, to be reconciled to God, that we may be blessed of him, that we may be led of him, that we may know that we are going to be with him. How can I know God? I need to be forgiven, I am a sinner, we are all sinners; and I am ignorant, I need to be forgiven and I cannot do anything about it. But God has done it! That is the meaning of Paul's assurance. God has given his only begotten son to bear our sins in his own body on the tree. 'God hath laid on him the iniquity of us all.' It is 'by his stripes we are healed'. It is because his body was broken, his blood was shed, because Calvary is a fact, and the resurrection, as Paul says here, is a fact. *That* is the thing that leads to every blessing, and until you believe this message, you will never know any blessing.

What do we say about it all? Well, what I want you to say is this. I want you to join me and to join Isaac Watts in saying something like this:

> Almighty God, to Thee,
> Be endless honour done,
> The undivided Three,
> And the mysterious One;
> Where reason fails with all her powers,
> There faith prevails, and love adores.

'It is,' says Blaise Pascal, 'the supreme achievement of reason to bring us to see that there is a limit to reason.' 'Where reason fails with all her powers' – and do not detract from them – 'There [at that point] faith prevails, and love [which reason does not understand] adores'.

Repent! Admit and confess your ignorance, your sin, your failure, and believe the message of the gospel concerning the Lord Jesus Christ the son of God, and then you will begin to share this new life that even in prison can say, '*nevertheless* I am not ashamed: for I know whom I have believed, and am persuaded [I am certain] that he is able to keep that which I have committed unto him against that day'.

'It is well with my soul'!

Chapter Three

SUNDAY EVENING SERMON
26th April 1964

The Right Diagnosis

For the which cause I also suffer these things: nevertheless I am not ashamed: for I know whom I have believed, and am persuaded that he is able to keep that which I have committed unto him against that day (2 Tim. 1:12).

When we read these words which Paul wrote to Timothy, we must remember that, because of his strenuous labours for the gospel and because of his sufferings, he was a man who had become old before his time. He had founded many churches in different parts of the then known civilised world; he had begun a great work, but there he was in a precarious position in one of Nero's prisons, liable, as Timothy knew with foreboding, to be put to death at any moment. And he encourages Timothy, not by telling him to cheer up, but by pointing him to the gospel. I know, he says in effect, that I am in prison because of the things I preach: 'nevertheless I am not ashamed'. He does not mean by that merely that he is not ashamed of his gospel, he means that he had not been 'put to shame'. He is in no difficulty, he is not unhappy or in trouble. Quite the reverse! He uses this figure of speech called litotes in which a negative is used to emphasise a positive. Another illustration of this is to be found in Romans 1:16. The apostle says there, 'I am not ashamed of the gospel of Christ.' What he really means is, 'I am exulting in it, I am very proud of it.' We all sometimes make statements powerfully by using a negative, do we not? It is said to be the characteristic English mode of expression – that we do not use superlatives, but express ideas which are superlative by means of negatives. We say, 'I am not ashamed'. We mean, 'I am tremendously proud of . . .'. And that is what the apostle is saying here – 'I am not in trouble, I am not in difficulties, I am not wondering whether I have been wise and right in preaching the gospel. Quite the reverse! I am in a gloriously happy condition, because "I know [him in] whom I have believed, and am persuaded [I am certain] that he is able to keep that which I have committed unto him against that day".'

And we have seen that what enables a man to face all contingencies like that is the gospel – not a certain kind of temperament, not a philosophy, but a gospel which can be known and defined, and a gospel which is a revelation to which we must submit. I am what I am, says Paul in effect to Timothy, because of my faith, my belief in the gospel. He reminds Timothy of that. 'Timothy', he says, 'you must hold this fast, this "form of sound words" which I have delivered to you, you must hold on to that, you must be absolutely certain. That "deposit" of truth that was given you guard for all you are worth, then you will be all right. If you do not, you will be timorous, frightened, alarmed, panicky, even as you are at the present time.' Now that is the essential argument of the great apostle, and I say it is still our great recommendation of this gospel today.

Notice that I say the 'great recommendation' of the gospel. Do not misunderstand me. I am not here as a kind of salesman or representative of the Church, trying to improve it by getting your patronage. It is exactly the other way round. I am here to tell you of the blessing that God alone can give you. I am simply recommending in that sense because of this great gift which the gospel holds out to all men everywhere.

And we have seen that we believe this because there is an authority, and the authority is the authority of revelation. We know nothing about God apart from what we are told in the Bible – I mean in an ultimate sense. And therefore, as I have shown, we either trust our own reason or else we submit to this; as the apostle puts it: 'If any man among you seemeth to be wise in this world, let him become a fool, that he may be wise' (1 Cor. 3:18). What he means is that if you do submit yourself to the Bible you will be dismissed as a fool. Many will say, 'Why that man, where is he living? Doesn't he read the books? Doesn't he know anything about science? Is he still believing that old Bible message?' Let them say it, says Paul. They were saying that in the first century, but he says it is the only way to become wise. Submit to this and we will get real knowledge. 'The world by wisdom knew not God', and man knows no more today about the great fundamental questions of life than he did in the first century. This is still our only authority.

What then is the message of the Bible? What is this message given to us by the apostles, given to them by the Lord Jesus Christ and passed on by them. Hold it fast, Paul says to Timothy, this message that I gave unto you. And he says elsewhere that what he preached all the other apostles preached. There were no different views among the apostles about God and about salvation; they were all preaching the same message. Why? Because, they had been given it by the same person. It is what Paul calls, in verse eight, 'The testimony of our Lord' – which means, the testimony concerning our Lord, the message which was delivered to the apostle. Paul says, 'I delivered unto you first of all that which I also received'. A message was delivered to him and he delivered it to the people. He was nothing but the transmitting station. He was not the originator of the message. He was given it, and his apostolic authority, by the risen Lord from heaven. That is the thing that makes him an apostle. And then the Holy Spirit came upon him and in demonstration of the Spirit and of power he 'announced' and 'declared' the truth of God.

That is the message which we believe today. It is perfectly summarised for us in this very passage that we are looking at. The apostle gives us here a very wonderful summary of Christian doctrine. You will find it repeatedly in the New Testament. The apostles were very fond of giving synopses of Christian doctrine. They delighted in saying the whole thing all over again. Fancy this apostle writing to a preacher, Timothy, and reminding him of the elements of the gospel and of salvation. And he did it because he was wise enough to know that even the preacher gets into trouble when he forgets the fundamental truths of the gospel. And there are many preachers in trouble today because they have departed from the same basic truths. They do not know it but this is the message they need. We all need it.

So here we have one summary of it, and, of course, the early Church produced other summaries, too. As we have seen, the great creeds, the Apostles' Creed and so on are just summaries of Christian doctrine which hold before us the cardinal elements without which there is no Christianity. And that is the very thing that the apostle does at this point, and that is what you and I must consider together.

I emphasise this because the great principle outlined here by the apostle, the thing on which his whole position depends, can now be put in this form: There is nothing more fatal in life than to *start* with particular problems and to discuss them immediately and directly. That is, of course, what we all tend to do by nature. We are interested in our particular problems, and we ask our questions and we want a discussion about them, or about one of them in particular. We say, 'What has Christianity to say about this?' and so on. Now the answer of the Bible is that that is a fatal procedure. No particular question or problem can be understood according to the Bible except in terms of the whole. We do not start with a part, we start with the whole. The particular is only understood in the light of the general. This is, of course, an absolutely vital principle. I am so concerned about this that I hope you will forgive me if I use an obvious illustration.

To be over concerned with the particulars at the expense of the general or the whole is exactly like a doctor who is only interested in symptoms and is unconcerned about the disease. That, you can take it from me, is a very profound principle in medical practice. The patient is always interested in symptoms. Naturally! The patient does not know much about diseases, but he is very interested in his headache or the pain in his side, and all he wants is something to get rid of the headache or the pain. He is not interested in anything else. That is, of course, because of his ignorance of medical things. A symptom is not a disease, but a symptom is possibly a manifestation of a disease. The thing that is really important is not the symptom but the disease.

Symptoms are, if you like, the amazing provision of nature to guide the expert physician to a diagnosis of the disease. That is where the whole question of medical science comes in – that men began to observe that certain diseases displayed certain symptoms. So that you can start with a symptom and, if you know your job and handle it properly, it will lead you to the disease, and then the thing to be treated is the disease. You do not stop with just medicating symptoms. If you do, you will be doing a grievous injustice to your patient and he may eventually lose his life because of that. You can give him an injection of morphia; the pain has gone and all seems well. But all is not of necessity well; if it is a cancerous growth it goes on growing. The patient says, 'I have got more pain.' Give him another injection, and you can go on injecting and injecting and the patient thinks you are a very kind doctor, but he dies of cancer. The business of the doctor is not to give his injection but first of all to discover what is the cause of this thing, what it is that has led to this symptom. And he does not medicate the symptoms until he does know exactly what is causing this particular one, and then he is in a position to deal with it; and incidentally in dealing with the disease, he will get rid of the symptoms.

Now Christianity is exactly like that. It is difficult for us to grasp that, is it not? Let me give you another illustration. It is so difficult that even medical students find it a problem. A man feels he would like to become a doctor, but he has to spend a most wearisome first year in doing chemistry and physics and biology. 'What is the use of this?' he says. 'I want to be treating people.' But he is made to do these subjects. Then he has to spend – at least he used to at one time – eighteen months or so in doing anatomy and physiology, not looking at a patient at all, in terms of patients, but doing wearisome dissection discovering nerves and blood vessels and all sorts of things. Oh what an utter waste of time! Why cannot he be treating people and handling diseases? Well, you see the object, do you not? If you have not got a fundamental knowledge of anatomy and physiology and so on, and if you do not know something about the working of life and drugs and things like that, and certain principles in chemistry and even in physics, you will not be able to be a good doctor. You must have a background of knowledge, and only then can you relate everything into that. If you do not know your anatomy and if you do not know how these anatomical structures function and work, you will not really be able to diagnose, not to interpret the symptoms. You have to go a great way back, you have got to discuss a great whole before you can really bring your mind to bear in an intelligent manner upon some particular part or problem.

Now, all that is a perfect illustration of what the gospel teaches and what the apostle Paul is teaching Timothy at this particular point. My friends, the individual problems of life can only be understood in the light of the whole problem. A man comes to me with a particular problem and says, 'Why this? Why that? Why does this happen to me?' Now, if I answer him immediately and directly I am being a very bad spiritual physician. A man comes to me and says, 'You are a Christian, you are a pastor of a church, I want some help from you.' Now, I cannot help him on those terms. The first thing I want to know is whether or not this man is a Christian. If he is a Christian I at once know the line on which I can deal with him and help him; if he is not, I really cannot help that man until he becomes one. I cannot medicate his symptoms until the disease has been dealt with. I cannot answer him his particular question unless he accepts the total view of life, death and eternity which the gospel provides.

This is the tremendous question. People today are concerned about particulars. I believe the world is in its present predicament politically and socially, with all its moral problems and everything else, for one main reason, and that is, that we have forgotten first principles, we have forgotten the fundamental postulate. We are missing the wood because of the trees, and the result is we are going entirely wrong. Take one illustration of this – the whole problem and question of moral delinquency, so called, and of juvenile delinquency. They are setting up commissions, royal commission after royal commission, and trying to examine and to investigate. They thought it was due to poverty; now, they say it is due to affluence – and so on – but you see they are wrong every time because they do not ask the fundamental question.

What we should be asking is – what is man? Why does anybody want to behave like that? These are the fundamental questions. But we do not face them, because we rush to the particulars. We must go back. Before I can answer your question of 'What is wrong with the world?' I have got to make you face this question – what is the world? Where has it come from? What is it meant to be like? And before I can answer your particular questions about man and his behaviour and misbehaviour, I must ask you to face another question with me – what is man? What is he meant to be like? What is he doing in this world? What is life itself?

So, then, the whole tragedy of the modern age, the whole confusion of the modern man, I suggest to you, is due to the fact that he is in too much of a hurry. He wants to have a kind of penny-in-the-slot machine. You put in your coin and you get what you want, and there it is – we are all in a desperate hurry. But we must stop and think! And the gospel is here in the world above everything else to call men to do just that. We have not got ready-made answers to all the questions: It is not a ready-reckoner view of life. Here is a great profound view of everything, and your particular question and problem can only be dealt with in the light of the whole.

That, then, is just my way of putting to you what the apostle put to Timothy. What he is saying is this: 'Timothy, get back to first principles. Do not consider me and my death and what is going to happen. Get back to the fundamentals, get back to the Lord himself and all he has done and all he has said. Get there and stay there, then you will never be troubled.' That is always the way. So, as we try to understand what makes a man say in prison and face to face with death, 'nevertheless I am not ashamed: for I know whom I have believed,' we must start with the great questions: what is life? What is the world? What is man? What is it all about? I cannot tell you what one particular thing means until we are agreed as to what the whole is all about.

So we start with question number one – what is this world and life in which we find ourselves? Here is what somebody said about it:

> All the world's a stage,
> And all the men and women merely players;
> They have their exits and their entrances;
> And one man in his time plays many parts,
> His acts being seven ages . . .

Then he goes through the seven ages and he ends with this:

> . . . Last scene of all,
> That ends this strange eventful history,
> Is second childishness, and mere oblivion,
> Sans teeth, sans eyes, sans taste, sans everything.

I have quoted Shakespeare, but was he right? Is that life? Is that it? Do you just start as a baby and go through the seven ages and end in that more or less gibbering condition and then – nothing? Is that life, is that the world, is that man? If it is, then my whole answer about the particular things that are happening is dependent upon that. You ask me about the bomb, about war, about theft and robbery and misdemeanours and so on. Well, my answer is going to be determined by my total view, if that Shakespeare passage is the truth – and that is the truth held by most people today. There is only one inevitable result, and that is the modern confusion, and, I suggest, for the following reasons.

What, then, are the views about life? In the last analysis there are only two possible views. There are what we may call the non-biblical (or the extra-biblical) view and the biblical view. I am referring now to these great questions about the world, life, man, death, what lies beyond – the whole thing. Now the non-biblical view, of course, is based upon nothing but speculation. Pure speculation! Just what a man says, what he thinks, a theory a man puts forward. Everything is based on reason, as we have seen, and what it comes to is this. People say that the world is really an accident. I am not caricaturing this. God forbid that I should – the thing is much too serious. But the view is that the world is literally an accident, and purely a matter of chance. We all know the theory about the two stars and how they passed too near one another at a given point and one knocked a piece off the other which fell into space and eventually became the cosmos. Accident! Chance! You can talk, if you like, about evolution, but, what it all comes to in the end is that everything is to be explained in terms of some great force – not a personal mind, but an impersonal force, with no understanding and no reason. A Frenchman once called it the 'élan vital' but it is just force. That is all it means still, and also that everything is the result of the operation of this force. That is the essence of the non-biblical view. There are endless variations of course, but that is what they all come to.

Now I say that these explanations are inadequate and to be rejected because they do not, of course, explain to us the ultimate origin. When I am told about these two stars, I want to know where they came from; or if I am told that there was just some sort of original gas, I ask, where did that come from? They do not know and they cannot tell us. There is no adequate explanation of ultimate origin.

But not only that; these theories are so totally inadequate to explain the facts and the phenomena by which we are confronted. Look at the order in nature; look at what we call the laws of nature, and their amazing regularity – spring, summer, autumn, winter; look at the design and all that you see in flowers, in animals and so on; the symmetry, the perfection and all these things. Now I say that force, accident, chance, or evolutionary process do not account for it; the thing is too perfect, too wonderful, and too extraordinary.

That leads me to another argument which has always to me seemed almost irrefutable, and that is the subtlety, the wonder and the balance in certain things that one finds in nature. I have always argued that the human eye alone is more than enough for me to prove that there is a God, a creator. This delicate, sensitive organ, so refined, able to discriminate as it does, this little organ which so governs the whole of our life in almost every respect. Is this accident? No, the whole thing is so perfect; it is such a perfect instrument, beyond anything that man could possibly make, that it postulates a great Mind, a great Designer, a great Artist.

But that is just putting in my words what the late Sir James Jeans, the scientist, came to at the end of his life, when he said he had come to the conclusion that at the back of everything there must be a great Mind; or, as somebody put it, that 'God is a great mathematician.' The mere facts of nature, I say, cannot be explained in terms of a blind, mechanical, unintelligent force. We know something about blind force. We see it in a fire, in an avalanche, or some such thing. What does it produce – order? No! Disaster! These explanations are not adequate.

And then when you come to ask, 'Is there a purpose in it all?' the answer they give is that there is none. If you really want to base your whole view of life and to answer your individual questions and solve your individual problems in terms of scientific humanism, then listen to one of the leading scientific humanists, Sir Julian Huxley, and he will tell you quite honestly that there is no object or end or purpose in the whole of life – none at all! It is all accident and you have no idea what may happen. There is no end or object or design.

Now that is inevitably the view of life outside the Bible. The Bible itself describes such a view in Acts 14, where we read a description of what the pagan world was like. (We have seen it earlier in Athens – even in Athens!) They had to fall back upon the gods, and here in Lystra when they found Paul and Barnabas performing a miracle, they said, 'These men are gods; one is Jupiter, one is Mercurius; Paul the speaker must be Mercurius,' and they attempted to worship them. That is the world, you see, without God. Everything is accident and chance or fate or luck, and there may be unseen gods at the back of it all. Life! – that is all it comes to. It is just a mystery, just an enigma. Is there purpose? None at all. Is there hope? Simply none – no hope at all. If we have a bad time in this world, well, it is bad luck, we must try to make the best we can of it or else we will fall into a state of cynicism. Walter Savage Landor, a very able man of the Victorian era, had adopted all these ideas and he became a cynic, and this is how he expressed his philosophy of life:

> I strove with none; for none was worth my strife;
> Nature I loved, and, next to nature, art;
> I warmed both hands before the fire of life;
> It sinks, and I am ready to depart.

That is life, you see, if you take it without God and without the biblical revelation, without this 'testimony of God' that the apostle Paul preached everywhere. 'I strove with none' – why not? – because, 'none was worth my strife'. There is a bit of conceit mixed up with the cynicism. It is not worth fighting, nobody is worth fighting. What do you live on? Well, 'Nature I loved' – beautiful scenery; I got something out of it, it made me feel happy for a while, when I got away out of the dusty, dirty cities up on to a mountain top. Then, 'Nature I loved, and, next to nature, art' the artist is able to help me a good deal and I must say I have had a fairly good time. 'I warmed both hands before the fire of life' and I had a wonderful time. Mid-day there was a great blaze, and at tea time it was still there and I was warming my hands, we were all happy together. But the fire is going out and, do what I will, I cannot stop it. The artist cannot stop it, nature cannot stop it. The fire is sinking, I am getting old, the end is coming. 'It sinks' All right you can go out as a gentleman – 'And I am ready to depart'. But you do not know where you are going, you have no hope. It has all come to an end. What is there in it? Is it worth all the fuss and bother?

And all that leads not only to cynicism but ultimately to

despair and suicide – it is not worth it. If there is nobody
worth fighting, in a sense life is not worth living. If things go
wrong why should you stand up against them? And you are
left in the end without an answer. You do not know, but you
have certain fears. Thoughts of 'the undiscovered country,
from whose bourn, no traveller returns'. But for that, with my
'native hue of resolution', I would soon solve the problem.
But . . . ! So I do not.

There, then, is the commonly accepted view. Let us turn to
the other and look at the biblical view. This is the thing that
the Bible teaches, this was the message that Paul taught, this
is what made him the man he was. This is a philosophy that
sees a man not only through life, but through death and the
beyond, and makes him ready and satisfied whatever may
come; so that he does not slink out, he sings, he exults, he
rejoices, he is more than conqueror, and he looks forward in a
way that nobody else does.

Let us then consider the great teaching of the apostle, and
that of the Bible everywhere. Take again that story of Paul
and Barnabas in Lystra. When the people there had seen Paul
performing a miracle, they said, 'This man must be a god, let
us worship him,' and they were on the verge of doing so.
'Stop!' said Paul in effect. 'Sirs, I beseech you, do not behave
in this foolish manner.' He said, 'You are doing this, of
course, because you have been worshipping idols, you are
afraid of life, you do not understand. So you have invented
gods, you have made idols to try to give yourselves some
explanation, and you are worshipping yourselves though you
do not know it; you think you are worshipping God. But these
are vanities, they are empty, there is nothing there.' 'Listen,'
he said, and he began to preach the living God to them. Was
not that in effect what he was saying? This is the whole
message of the Bible. Read those words of the apostle there in
Lystra, as they form such a perfect summary of what the
gospel has to say to this modern world of ours. 'Sirs, why do ye
these things? We also are men of like passions with you, and
preach unto you that ye should turn from these vanities unto
the living God, which made heaven, and earth, and the sea,

and all things that are therein' – and he went on to expound
this *living God* to them.

So, that is the biblical message. This book called the Bible is
the great manual of the soul, it is the textbook of life. Here is a
book which really does answer our questions. How does it do
that? Well, see how it begins. It does not say, 'Are you not
feeling well' or 'Do you want healing?' 'Are you feeling
lonely, do you want a friend?' or 'Do you want a bit of
happiness and joy? Come along!' No that is the way of cults.
That is not the Bible. The Bible is different. We have a
problem, and we begin to read . . . 'In the beginning God . . .
That is the Bible. You see the Bible never starts with man – it
always starts with God. And the whole trouble with the
modern world is that it starts with man and ends with man,
and so it ends in confusion and chaos. But the essence of the
biblical message is to say that there is no hope until the world
stops and starts again, and starts with God, because you
cannot understand the world itself, leave alone man and
the problems of the world and man, until you have started
with God. Where has the world come from? The Bible
says – God! 'In the beginning God created the heaven and
the earth . . .'.

Now, the Bible does not argue about the being and the
existence of God. It declares it. It asserts it. I know that
certain Christian philosophers down the ages have tried to
produce proofs of the existence of God. They are all right as
far as they go. They are a great help to people who already
believe in God, but they very rarely convince anybody else.
They are worth noting, but I am not going to go into them in
detail. There are certain arguments, I have already given you
one – the argument from nature if you like, the design and
the order and so on – the cosmological argument. But there
are other arguments, such as the one about the uncaused
cause. Every effect has a cause, but that in turn is the effect of
another cause. And back and back and back you go until you
arrive at the uncaused cause. That is God! Or, if you like, a
kind of moral argument – we recognise, all of us, that there is
Bad – Good – Better. But Bad – Good – Better suggests

Best. Where is it? Not to be found in this world, not to be found in man. That is God! The ultimate – and so on. These are the arguments, and the very fact that they have argued, that you can think about him at all is, in a strange way, a proof in and of itself that he is there – the ontological argument. But do not worry about these arguments. All I am saying is that they are there and you can use them if you like, but they are not enough. What is the ultimate proof? The ultimate proof is the revelation of God himself. That is the case of the Bible. God has said certain things about himself and in history he has proved that they are true. That is the biblical case.

Let me work it out for you merely in outline by putting it like this. The Bible is ultimately a book about God. 'Ah,' you say, 'but I thought it dealt with the human race and with kings and queens and births and marriages and deaths and wars.' Yes, you are perfectly right. But you see all this under God! The Bible is a book about God, and it is not a book which claims that as the result of a lot of meditation and research it has 'arrived' at a belief in God. That is the popular modern theory, which is pure theory, evolutionary theory applied to the realm of the spiritual.

What the Bible writers say is that God spoke! They do not say he 'arrived'. God spoke! And they tell us exactly what he told them. They say that God is a triune God. 'Dear me,' says someone, 'fancy saying that in this day and age. I have come to you because I am in trouble and because I want a little bit of help, I want an answer to my question, I am asking you to solve my problem, and are you going to preach to me about the triune God?' 'My dear sir,' he says, 'don't you know where you are living, don't you know what your world is like? We have not the leisure today to sit back and indulge in this abstruse theology about the blessed Holy Trinity.' Haven't you? I am here primarily just to say this; that the only hope for this world at this moment is the fact that there is a triune God, that this is not the only world, and that all we know about this world is not the whole truth, indeed it is very little. Above it, beyond it, is the triune God – Father, Son, Holy Spirit. I hope later to try to expound this great doctrine to you still further and in greater detail. I am simply giving you a summary of it now. But there it is, this fundamental statement of the Bible, one God in father, son and Holy Spirit, and he tells us something about himself. He tells us that he is eternal, that he is 'from eternity to eternity,' that he is glorious, which means that he is absolutely perfect, and so glorious and so perfect that we cannot conceive of it. Glory is the ultimate attribute of God – and that is something ineffable, something that baffles description. He is also holy. God is holy, God is just, God is righteous. God is power, omnipotent, all-powerful. He is wise, he knows everything. He is love, he is mercy and compassion. He has taught men these things. He has come to his servants and said: 'This is the message, tell the people, I am such and such a God,' and has revealed himself and these glorious attributes.

But the one thing I am particularly concerned about here, of course, is that he is a God who has a plan and a purpose. Did you notice how Paul puts it here to Timothy? He says: 'Be not thou therefore ashamed of the testimony of our Lord, nor of me his prisoner: but be thou partaker of the afflictions of the gospel according to the power of God; who hath saved us, and called us with an holy calling, not according to our works, but according to his own purpose' – his own purpose! – 'and grace, which was given us in Christ Jesus before the world began.' This is to me the whole secret of everything. That this universe of ours is not an accident, it is not the result of chance. It is something that has come into being as the result of the purpose and the plan of the triune God, 'before the world began'. God in eternity decided, chose, elected, determined, to create a world. The world is not an accident. It is not the result of the interaction of blind forces. It is something that he decided to make and to create – 'In the beginning God created'. There it is!

See, too, how the apostle Paul argues about that very thing in Romans 1:18ff: 'For the wrath of God is revealed from heaven against all ungodliness and unrighteousness of men, who hold the truth in unrighteousness; because that which may be known of God is manifest in them; for God hath shewed it unto them. For the invisible things of him from the foundation of the world are clearly seen . . . even his eternal power and godhead; so that they are without excuse.' What he means is that if men only had eyes to see, they would see the marks of God and the proofs of God in what he has made, the invisible things, his power and his godhead, his creator-hood. It is there if you can only see it – the marvel, the wonder, the perfection, the balance. God! He made every-thing in the beginning, he started time, he made a perfect world and a perfect man in it. He made angels, unseen spiritual persons. He made heaven and the earth, the animals; he made man, he made everything, and it was all good and perfect.

Now, *that* is how the Bible leads you to face your particular problem. You start with the whole origin of the cosmos. Then you say to me, 'Well, that sounds very wonderful, but it does not look like the world in which I find myself today. It is not very perfect. I find everything which is imperfect. I find strife and envy and jealousy and war and bitterness and drunken-ness and faithlessness. I find the world a chaos and yet you say God made it perfect. Have you not something to say at that point?' Oh yes, indeed I have, and the Bible has a great deal to say. It tells us that some of the angels, whom God created perfect and to whom he gave absolute free will, rebelled against God in their pride because they wanted to be God; that they fell and that they have influenced the whole uni-verse. That is the devil, and that is the fall of man. You say, 'Do you believe things like that today?' My dear friend, today's world is what drives me to believe in it. I do not see a world going upwards, but a world going downwards. I do not understand life apart from the doctrine of the fall, the doc-trine of evil, the doctrine of hell, the doctrine of the devil. It is all here in this book. The Bible explains it. It is not accident and chance. God made the world in that perfect manner and it is as it is because of the devil and evil and his influence upon this world of ours.

But – and again let me say this is nothing but summarising at this point – the Bible goes on to say more. And this is where the hope comes in. The world, we have seen, is as it is because of the devil, because of the fall. Is there any hope? Is there in philosophy? Is there in politics? Is there an evolutionary process? It does not look like it, does it? And, of course, there is not. The world goes round in circles – better, worse; better, worse; up and down. Look at secular history and you will see this – a constant cycle, as if we are going to arrive and we never do, and then back we go, with always a dark age following an age of enlightenment – round and round in circles.

Is there no hope? There is! And here is the hope, that the triune God is still interested in this world; that God did not abandon it when man fell in his folly and listened to the devil and became the dupe of the devil. God is still interested! The doctrine of deism, which means that God made the universe like a watchmaker making a clock, winding it up, and then putting it down and having nothing more to do with it, is absolutely wrong. God is not only transcendent he is Immanent, and he is concerned and he is involved. Not only that; the whole story of the Bible is that God is still controlling the world. That, far from abandoning it, God is interested in it and is controlling it and is acting upon it. He does so in his providence, but he does so in a still more definite manner. There is a great phrase – you will often find it in the Bible: 'When the fulness of the times was come' – What does it mean?

It means that God has a purpose for this world. The devil has tried to spoil it but he is not going to succeed. He has succeeded temporarily. God in his infinite wisdom has given him that liberty. I do not know why. Do not ask me; I cannot explain. That is the mind of God. But God has allowed evil, he has allowed the devil, and the fall, but he is not going to allow it to go on. God is still interested. He is still concerned, he is still intervening. How do I know? I point you to the flood, or to a man called Abram, who was living as a pagan in a place called Ur of the Chaldees. God went to that man and said, Come out! I want to make a man of you, I want to make a nation, a people of you. I am going to influence this whole world through you, I am going to save it ultimately through you and your seed. Abraham! God acting! That is what Abraham said. He did not claim he had had an idea; he said that God had visited him and had called him. And out of him came the Jews. The whole story of the Jews is but a great revelation of God, his character, and his power. Look at them! Look at their victories! How did they get them? Was it their military prowess? No, they always ascribed it to God. When they got defeated – what was the matter? They had forgotten God. Their whole history is to be understood in terms of God. And, once again, there is the whole question of prophecy, which we dealt with earlier.

In other words, for me to conclude here, nothing is more important for us as we try to understand the problems of life and to solve them, than to recognise that there are two types of history. There is the history that God permits, and there is that which God produces. There is the history of what man does in his folly and the trouble into which he gets himself, and there is the history of the intervention of God; of God acting through Israel, doing things to the nations that were against them, and ultimately when the fulness of the times had come, sending this blessed person, 'Jesus Christ our Saviour,' to whom Paul refers, and to whom he tells Timothy to look. He sends him into this world. This is God. God's history!

And, according to this record, the message of this book, these two histories are going to go on, until eventually they coalesce, and there will be an end. The world is not an accident. It did not start as an accident, it will not end as one. You know, the bombs are not going to end the world – I can tell you that now. I make a prophecy. I stake the whole of Christianity on this: the world is not going to end as the result of a hydrogen or an atomic bomb. God is going to end the world. And the world will not end until that day of which Paul speaks. 'I know whom I have believed, and am persuaded that he is able to keep that which I have committed unto him against that day'! The end! God who started it will end it, and he will end it perfectly, and gloriously. Death is not the end, either for man or for animals or for the whole cosmos. There is to be a grand regeneration when the entire cosmos will be restored to its pristine perfection, and God will be over all and in all.

Now, this is what I am saying. It is in the light of all that that you understand your particular problem. Have you lost your health? Are you in trouble? Have you lost a loved one? What is your particular problem today? I say to you, if you want a satisfactory answer, put it into that context. That context! Thank God for it! This is not the only life, nor is it the only world. Death is not the end. God is over all. 'God liveth'! The living God, the true God, the only God, and all things are under his hands. And we can say with confidence with the great and mighty apostle Paul in Romans 8:18: 'I reckon that the sufferings of this present time are not worthy to be compared with the glory which shall be revealed in us.' But you can only be persuaded of that if you accept this message, if you accept the whole truth. You cannot get any particular benefit out of this gospel unless you believe the whole gospel about God the father, God the son, and God the Holy Spirit, and how they made the world and man and all, and how (blessed be the name of God) they are still interested and still concerned. I know of nothing that enables me to live today but this! That God so loved the world that he sent into it – 'He gave' – and even to the death on the cross, 'his only begotten son, that whosoever believeth in him should not perish but have everlasting life.' 'God was in [and through] Christ, reconciling the world unto himself.' It is in the light of that that your every problem is solved, your every question is answered. The vital question is – do you believe the gospel? Do not start with yourself. Start with yourself in the light of God if you like. Start with God and see yourself under him, and then believe the whole revelation and you will find peace and rest for your souls, you will have answers that you never dreamt of. You will 'see life steadily, you will see it whole'. More; you will see through death even to the eternity beyond and the glory everlasting. Believe the gospel! Hold it fast – this 'form of sound words'. And then you will be able to join this great man, and in whatsoever state you find yourself you will be able to say with him, 'nevertheless I am not ashamed: for I know whom I have believed, and am persuaded that he is able to keep that which I have committed unto him against that day'.

Chapter Four

SUNDAY EVENING SERMON
3rd May 1964

Who is Man?

For the which cause I also suffer these things: nevertheless I am not ashamed: for I know whom I have believed, and am persuaded that he is able to keep that which I have committed unto him against that day (2 Tim. 1:12).

As we look again at this great statement, let me remind you that it is important for us to remember the whole context, from verses six to fourteen, as we continue with our consideration of this particular verse. We have seen that far from feeling disappointed or unhappy, Paul, in prison, is filled with a spirit of exaltation and of joy. I hold this passage before you, therefore, because I suggest that this is the very essence of the Christian message. The Christian message is a message that is offered to us to enable us to live. This is not something theoretical, not just some philosophy up in the sky somewhere. There is nothing in the whole world that is more practical than this Christian message, this Christian gospel. It is not a theoretical view of life. The great thing about this is that it has proved in practice to be a mighty power enabling men to live in a worthy manner, and, especially, enabling them to do what it did to the apostle here, to become more than conqueror. It is a view which enables a man not only to look at life but to look at death, to look at eternity, and still triumph and prevail. It is this message that enables a man to look at life at its darkest and starkest and say, 'nevertheless I am not ashamed'.

And so I am preaching this gospel because it is the most practical thing under heaven at this moment. People think that it is remote; or that it is not applicable to life today, and is not realistic. I am here just to contend that nothing else does help us to live but this. We are living in a world in which we see everything else breaking down, and that is why I exhort men and women to listen to the gospel. And here we have it in the form of the personal experience of the great apostle Paul, and the question, for us, I say again, is – how can we live like that? Are we living in the way he did? Are we more than conquerors in this world, are we mastering life, are we going through triumphantly? Or are we merely shuffling through, being battered and buffeted and just managing to stand? Have we had to fall back on some philosophy of Stoicism or something like that, which is, ultimately, nothing but a philosophy of despair? Or have we stopped thinking altogether, have we given up the fight, saying, as many have said before us, 'Let us eat, drink, and be merry; for tomorrow we die.' What is the use of worrying, what is the use of reading or thinking? The great men cannot find an answer, who am I to find an answer? Don't waste your time, make the best of it. 'Gather ye rosebuds while ye may.' There are millions turning to that kind of thinking (or absence of thinking) at the present time.

The thing we must obviously discover, therefore, is what it is that enables a man like Paul to be able to utter this glorious 'nevertheless'. I have been trying to show you that he himself tells us in this context exactly how he did it, and we have been considering some of the reasons for his great certainty. We have seen that it is not a matter of temperament and that the apostle's gospel is still relevant to the twentieth century. I have tried to show you, too, that there is only one gospel and that we know nothing apart from what we have in this book. We can speculate, of course, and any one of us can do it almost as well as anybody else. But what authority have we, what sanction have we, what proof have we? We have none.

What do we really know about God apart from what we read in this book? Nature takes us so far, but it does not take us far enough. It does not bring us to a personal god, to a god of love and mercy and compassion. And yet that is what we all need. You can trace his marks in history, but again it is only power. There is no knowledge of God apart from what we have in this book. Now, we have already established that. We must submit to the message, because we do not receive the benefits unless we first of all take the message.

And that brings me to my next point, which is a very important one. Christianity has nothing to give to anyone who does not believe it. That is where so many go so wrong today. People say, 'Your gospel has been preached for two thousand years but look at the world!' – and they think that that is a conclusive argument. But of course that misses the whole point. As G. K. Chesterton once put it so perfectly: 'Christianity has not been tried and found wanting; it has been found difficult and not tried.' The world has not tried it! It seems to think that Christianity is a sort of teaching which can be applied as one would apply an Act of Parliament and so change the world. Christianity has never claimed to do that at all – not a word of that kind is to be found in the whole of the New Testament. No, we must take the gospel as it is found there. It does not offer anyone peace, it does not offer anyone joy, or mastery over life and triumph over circumstances, until and unless you believe it, and believe it as a whole, and believe in that blessed person who makes it what it is. You get no benefits from Christianity until you believe its central message. All these things that come to us as experiences are, as it were, the results that follow from our central committal of ourselves to it.

So that it seems to me that the position we have arrived at is this: I say we cannot get any blessings until we believe the message of the gospel. So what is the message about? In order to answer this we have seen that we must submit to the biblical method as well as the biblical message. The Bible wants us to know the truth, the whole truth. So before we start with our own particular problems and those of the world, we must be sure that we know what the world is and the Bible tells us that there is only one adequate explanation of the world and that is that it has been created by God. It is not an accident, it is not the result of chance, it is not something fortuitous but rather, 'In the beginning God created . . .'. He not only created, he controls, he sustains and he intervenes in it. He acts in the world, because he has a plan and a purpose. 'Who hath saved us, and called us with an holy calling, not according to our works, but according to his own purpose and grace, which was given to us in Christ Jesus before the world began.'

There you have the biblical view of the world and of life in general. God started the time process, he is controlling it, and he is going to end it. That is the message. And God has a great purpose. I would say once more that to me this is the most thrilling discovery a man can ever make; that there is a purpose in life and in this world, and that the whole thing is not 'a tale told by an idiot, full of sound and fury, signifying nothing'. It is not that. 'Life is real, life is earnest; And the grave is not its goal.' The whole cosmos has got an end, and the purpose of God is at the back of everything. Now that is the first fundamental statement.

It seems to me, therefore, that the next vital question for us is the one – what is man? 'If you say,' says somebody, 'that the whole universe, the whole cosmos, has a purpose and an end and an object and that it is in the hand of God who is bringing his great purposes to pass, where, then, does man come in, in all this?' I would suggest that it is only common sense to say that there is no object or point or purpose in considering the problems of man until we know what man is. Obviously our answer to the problems and questions is going to be determined by our view of man. But that is the tragedy today; people are ignoring the *fundamental* questions. We are living in a world of activism. Everybody is rushing here and there to solve some particular problem or other, but the great question is never faced: what is man? What is he doing here in this world? Where has he come from? Is there any point in his existence? Obviously, these are the great questions that must be considered at once, and the apostle does so here in a very

plain and in a very clear manner, as I want to show you. This is
indeed one of the great messages of the Bible. The Bible tells
us the truth about man, and then when we have understood
the truth about him, we shall have light upon the things that
happen to him, and on the only way in which he can be
delivered.

The ancient Greek philosophers asked this question –
what is man? They were very wise and able men, and very
profound thinkers, and, having ruminated over life and its
attendant circumstances, they came to the conclusion that the
essence of wisdom is to 'know thyself'! They said that this was
man's great problem, his biggest question: 'know thyself'.
How many people really know themselves? Of course we
think we do, but we do not. We are dishonest with ourselves,
we paint wonderful pictures of ourselves, we defend ourselves
and so on, yet we do not really know ourselves; and most of
our troubles are due to this fact. The Greeks said that we must
start there – 'know thyself', but the question for us is: how am
I to do that? How can a man know himself? Have you ever
tried it? If you try, you will find that it is a terrible problem, to
know one's self.

The modern world is full of this attempt on the part of man
to understand himself and to answer the question, what is
man? I am not going to weary you with the various current
popular theories, because you are familiar with them. But one
of the most popular today is that man is just a biological being,
that is this mysterious body of ours and all the discoveries of
the last hundred years, such as our ductless glands, and other
things, vital to life. These are the things, I must tell you
incidentally, that the scientists of a hundred years ago were
dismissing with absolute confidence as completely useless
vestigial remains. Now they find that they are essential to life,
and people have gone to the other extreme and are saying that
man is really what he is as the result of the various proportions
of thyroid, pituitary, suprarenal glands, and the various
others.

Another view is more philosophical and says that man
is – how shall I put it – simply the result of the interplay of

dialectical forces. Man is what he is as the result of supply and demand, political forces and so on. Then there is another, more sociological, view of man which explains him entirely in terms of his environment and the particular social background in which he is brought up. Indeed there are some who believe that what determines what a man is, is geography, even climate. You are familiar with that, are you not? The nearer you get to the equator, they say, the softer people are and the milder, the more emotional. The further away you get from the equator and nearer you get to the North or the South Pole the harder, more intellectual, more resistant and less emotional they are. So you see it is all a question of the lattitude on which you have been born and on which you have been brought up. These are put forward quiet seriously.

Another very popular explanation of man's identity is the psychological one. Freud started it; it governs novels, and it governs the treatment of delinquents; it has made its way into the prisons, indeed, it is governing almost everything, including education. This view sees man in terms of instincts, and, to those who hold it, man is but a bundle of impulses and drives, an aggregate, a collection of the forces and powers that are inside him.

Now, I wonder whether these views satisfy you. Many of them, of course, contradict one another and are mutually exclusive. Some of them are optimistic, some are pessimistic. There are some people who have come to the conclusion that man is hopeless. They see no purpose in his life, they cannot prophesy any end, nor do they see any end in history or in man. Some of the greatest historians have said that they see no line, no objective, nothing moving in a given direction. They do not believe in 'one far-off divine event to which the whole creation moves'. No, they say, it is either going round and round in circles or it is all pure accident and chance.

But what is more or less common to all of these theories is the idea that man in reality is nothing but an animal. They may say that he is a reasoning animal; they may make great play of the fact that man's cerebrum has developed much more than any other animal, but to them he is still only an

animal. He may be the highest form of animal life, nevertheless he is still only an animal, and that is how we must think of
him. And indeed all those various theories can be reduced to
that common denominator. But do they really satisfy us? Are
these explanations adequate? Do they really account for man
as we know him, even as we know ourselves, in so far as we
can know ourselves?

Then again, do they account for the amazing contradiction
that is to be seen in man? What a contradiction he is, and
modern man in particular. Never has man shown the contra-
dictions in his nature more clearly than he is doing at the
present time. Look at man from one angle and you will say he
is great, he is noble, he is wonderful! But then take another
look at him and you say that he is small, vile, ignoble, and
ugly. And the two things are, of course, perfectly true. Man is
a contradiction. Look at the very century in which we live and
you can see the whole thing quite plainly. On the one hand
you have the phenomenal achievements of modern man, the
amazing scientific discoveries and their development. This
century has been an astounding one, with man revealing the
greatness of his power and his understanding; but remember,
it has also been the century of Buchenwald and of other
concentration camps. It is the century of the bombs and of the
two most devastating wars that the world has ever known; it is
the century of divorce and infidelity, of ugliness and foulness,
and of rapacity and greed and vice. The same century! The
same man! This extraordinary contradiction: greatness and
smallness, wisdom and folly, are all mixed up. There is a
central contradiction at the very heart of man, and all the
explanations given really do not account for it.

You remember what Shakespeare says about man: 'What a
piece of work is a man! How noble in reason! how infinite in
faculty! in form, in moving, how express and admirable! in
action how like an angel! in apprehension how like a god! . . .'
Man is a spectacle. That is Shakespeare's statement about
him, but is it the whole truth? Is it really man? 'What a piece
of work is a man! How noble in reason!' Are you seeing it at
the present time? How do you think the majority of people

are spending their time at this moment? Are they displaying
this ability of reason? Are they giving themselves to ponder-
ing the great questions of life and death and eternity, and all
the problems of man? 'Noble in reason!' Is he? 'Infinite in
faculties!' Is he displaying that today? 'In form, in moving,
how express and admirable! in action, how like an angel!
in apprehension, how like a god!' Is man displaying these
qualities?

No, I say, this is a partial picture and Shakespeare, to be
quite fair to him, shows the other side too, and more or less
dismisses him as a fool. He saw the two things and they have
always been in man. And you do not describe man truly and
accurately until you describe him as a whole and give due
weight to the two sides.

So now I want to put before you the biblical view of man.
The apostle puts it here in this letter to Timothy in a very
interesting phrase. Come back to this great word of his: 'For
the which cause I also suffer these things: nevertheless I am
not ashamed: for I know whom I have believed, and am
persuaded' – I am perfectly certain, I am perfectly satisfied –
'that he is able to keep that which I have committed unto him
against [or until] that day.' What is this that he has committed
unto him? Now, in the answer to that question is the whole of
the biblical teaching with regard to man. It is what the Bible
calls *the soul*! The apostle says, 'I am in prison but I am not
ashamed and I am not troubled, I am not distressed.' Why?
'Because I have committed my soul and its safe-keeping into
the hands of Christ and I know he will keep it safe. Whatever
man may do to me, my soul is safe. The soul! "That which I
have committed unto him".'

This is, of course, the thing that makes man 'man'. This is
what differentiates him from the animals. Let me quote some
words to you, which are interesting because they were spoken
by T. H. Huxley, the grandfather of Sir Julian Huxley and his
brother Aldous Huxley. T. H. Huxley was not a Christian.
He was a great supporter of Charles Darwin and he propa-
gated Darwin's teaching perhaps more eloquently than anybody else, but he said this: 'Between man and the highest

beast there exists' (and here are his words) 'an enormous gulf, a divergence immeasurable and practically infinite.' And of course that is precisely what the Bible has always said about man.

And what is it that makes man so different? The answer is that man is a creature whom God has made in his own image and likeness. God made the animals, yes, but not in his own image and likeness. Man is essentially different. He is not just an animal, he is a man. That means that he has an intellectual and a moral and a religious nature. Man has not only the power of intellect, he has the power of self-examination, self-reflection; he can look at himself, analyse himself and speak about himself. The animal cannot do that, man can. He has been given this intellectual power which is in God himself. God gave something of that to man – intellect! his intellectual power and capacity!

Then God gave man a moral nature. You can, of course, train a dog to do, or not to do, many things. You can teach him good manners as you can various other animals, but you can never make an animal a moral being. It acts instinctively. It can learn that if it does a forbidden thing it gets punished, and it will stop doing it. Pavlov has gone into all that and scientists and others are now trying to treat men like Pavlov's dogs. But the point I am establishing is that one can never make an animal into a moral being, one cannot give him a moral nature and the capacity for moral reflection, moral judgment, and moral determinations.

And then above all, of course, man has a religious character. 'Man', says somebody, 'is a worshipping animal.' I don't like that. Man worships because he is man, he is not a 'worshipping animal'. But man has this sense of the eternal. There is in every man a sense of God, a sense of something beyond. Both archaeologists, and anthropologists in particular have been able to produce irrefutable evidence to prove that even the most primitive races all have a sense of a supreme, high god. Some of them are animists, and worship spirits in trees for instance; some are idolaters; but all of them, even the most primitive, have a sense of a great, supreme, high, god. It is innate in human nature. Man has got a religious nature.

The Bible says he has all this because he has been made in the image and the likeness of God, and the thing that makes man *man* is this particular characteristic – in other words, man is body, soul, spirit. Or, if you prefer it, man is body and soul. You may say that the spirit is a section of the soul; I am not concerned to quarrel about that at this point. All I would say here is, that man has an animal part of his nature – a body. The body is very similar to that of the animal. But what makes man man is this other aspect, the power and capacity that he has, not only for self-reflection and communication with others, but above all for God, this spiritual element, this something within him that tells him – and again I quote Longfellow – that 'Dust thou art, to dust returnest, was not spoken of the soul'. It is this thing in man that cries out for 'an ampler ether, a diviner air'; this thing that tells man, as the book of Ecclesiastes puts it, that God has placed eternity in his heart; this thing in man that tells him that he is bigger than the world, that he is meant for something beyond himself – *this* is the soul.

This is, I repeat, what makes man man – that over and above his bodily animal part there is this other part, unseen and intangible but of which we are all aware. A man cannot think of himself as going out of existence. You may think or say that when you die it is the end, but you cannot believe that, or even imagine it, because there is something about us that suggests we are immortal, that man was not made to die. We know that there is this other element in us which is imperishable. And this is the essence of the biblical teaching. Here the apostle says, 'I am as I am, and I am able to say "nevertheless" because I know my *soul* is safe. Let them do what they like to my body, they cannot touch my soul,' he says. It is the fact that he knows he has got a soul that really gives him the confidence that he shows here.

Now it is not confined to the apostle Paul of course; he only received this teaching from our Lord and Saviour Jesus Christ, his master, who once put it like this: 'What shall it profit a man though he gain the whole world and lose his own soul?' On another occasion he used a parable. He told a story about a very rich man. This man was so wealthy and had done so well that his success had even become an embarrassment to him, and his barns were now too small to hold all his goods. So he said, 'Now what shall I do? I will pull down these barns and I will build greater, and then I will say to myself, "Soul, thou hast much goods laid up for many years; take thine ease, eat, drink, and be merry." But God said unto him, "Thou fool, this night thy soul shall be required of thee: then whose shall these things be, which thou hast provided?"' He had forgotten the soul! Our Lord was always teaching this. He did so again in the Parable of Dives and Lazarus. In that story, the trouble with the rich man is that he has forgotten that he has a soul. This is the whole of the teaching of the Bible. It starts with it – man created in the image of God, more than animal, a living soul with a capacity for God and for eternity. This is the essence of man, and this is what makes man man.

I am not surprised that the modern world is as it is, in trouble and perplexity, full of despair and of hopelessness. Modern man does not know what 'man' is! How can he know what has gone wrong if he does not know what he is; how can he put things right if he is wrong in his whole conception of himself? There is the first thing, but let me hurry on.

What was man meant to do in this world, what was he meant to be? I think that is a very urgent question for this generation, is it not? What is man here for? Is man merely an animal? Is he just in the world to eat and to drink and indulge his sex – is that it? Is that what man is for? Is that man's life? No, says the Bible, man, being made in the image and the likeness of God, was meant to be the lord of creation, he was meant to be God's representative in this world. That is why God gave to him the privilege of naming all the animals. He was meant to rule over them and to govern them. We are seeing him doing that now to some degree, and yet at the same time, because he is what he is, he is being governed by them in turn. There is a perpetual warfare – man's mastery, man's slavery. But he was meant to be master, the lord of creation, he was meant to live to the glory of God. Let me quote again that great answer in the Shorter Catechism of The Westminster Confession. The first question is this: 'What is the chief end of man?' And the answer: 'The chief end of man is to glorify God and to enjoy him for ever.' That is what man was meant to do! Is man doing it?

Then let me go on to the next question. What was meant to determine man's happiness in this world? We all want to be happy. Nobody likes and enjoys trouble. Man was meant to be happy and to enjoy the fruit of the earth; he was meant to live a full life and to be in a state of contentment. God made him and put him in a place called Paradise, and that is what it was meant to be. What is intended, then, to determine man's happiness? And here is the very essence and nerve of the biblical diagnosis of man and his troubles at this moment. Man's happiness was never meant to be determined by his circumstances, and that is the fatal blunder that we all tend to make. We think circumstances determine happiness, so most of us think, like the man I have already quoted, that what makes a man happy is to have plenty of money, and that we can buy happiness. But we cannot. We can buy pleasure but we cannot buy happiness. We can be multi-millionaires and still be miserable; we cannot buy happiness! Some millionaires are well known, and one of them was honest enough to admit that he was a great failure in life. I think that he has tried marriage five times already but he still does not know what it is to be a happily married man – and he is the richest man in the world! You see, we cannot buy it. Money is very useful but our happiness in this world is not determined by it, nor by goods, nor by possessions. No, no! Man, because he is what he is, can only be happy in another dimension. As long as man is dependent upon circumstances he is going to be miserable.

You see, that is where people go wrong today. They think that if only we could banish bombs, and put an end to war, if only we could do away with prisons or put in some new treatment, if only we were all educated, or if only we had plenty of money and could have plenty of drink, and plenty of dancing, and plenty of sex then we should be perfectly happy. And it has never worked. Why? Because our circumstances will generally be against us. Man's happiness depends on one thing only – and that is his relationship to God! That is the only thing. St. Augustine, that brilliant philosopher, came at long last to see it, having tried everything, philosophy, a mistress, and all the rest in order to find peace and happiness and rest. 'Thou hast made us for thyself, and our souls are restless until they find their rest in thee.' We cannot get it anywhere else. We must come back to the soul and to God who made it. We were made for him, we are meant for him, we have a correspondence with him, and we will never come to rest until, like that needle on the compass, we strike that northern point, and there we come to rest – nowhere else.

That leads inevitably to a further question which is that if all these are fundamental postulates with regard to man – and they are – why then, is man as he is, and why is life in this world as it is today? Why all these problems, why all these troubles, why all the restlessness and the heartache, why all the bustling attempt to find peace and rest and satisfaction in pleasure in various forms? What has gone wrong? Surely that is an important question. If I am to go through this world, able to say with the apostle 'nevertheless' to whatever happens, if I am to be happy in prison, and face to face with death and the end of all things as far as I am concerned, then I say I must know the answer to these great questions, every single one of them. What has gone wrong? Why is life as it is? Why is a man in prison for preaching the gospel? Why are there wars and rumours of wars? Why is there dishonesty? Why are vows broken? Why are little innocent children suffering, breaking their little hearts, not knowing a father or a mother's love, buffeted and thrown backwards and forwards by the selfishness of men and women? Why all this? And there is only one adequate explanation! It is the explanation in the Bible from beginning to end. Man was made in the image and likeness of God, but he rebelled against him, he became inflated with his own importance. He wanted to be as God so he deliberately defied God and broke his commandments and went his own way, and thus he fell.

And all this has led to the fact that man has lost the face of God, that he is out of correspondence with God, no longer knows God, and is no longer blessed by God. Man, you see, has turned his back upon God and has made himself a god. He has become egocentric. He tries to think that he is autonomous, that he has everything he needs within himself, that he is the centre of the universe and can plan life and the whole of the universe itself. But he finds that he cannot do that – and why not? The answer is perfectly simple according to this explanation. Man has lost his balance.

Now what I mean by lost his balance is this. Man, we have seen, was made body, soul and spirit, and as God made man, he had the spirit and the rational soul which enabled him to control his body. The body has its instincts and its desires. Man would not be a perfect man, even in a bodily sense, if he did not have these instincts. The idea, for example, that sex is sinful in and of itself, is utterly unbiblical; and those who taught in the past that sex was sinful per se did not know their Bible, or their Christianity. It was a false religion that made them teach it. No, God has made man like this and there is nothing wrong with our instincts. So, what is wrong?

Well, man, as he was made originally and perfectly, controlled his instincts. They were his servants and he used them not only to satisfy himself but supremely to the glory of God. Man was balanced and all was happy. He lived in the different spheres, on the different realms and there was a balance and a poise about his life. But the moment man disobeyed God, he lost his relationship to God. The highest faculty of all – the spirit – became dead and non-operative. Paul, in Ephesians 2:1, says, 'And you hath he quickened, who were dead in trespasses and sins.' He means that they were spiritually dead; they did not know God, they did not realise there was God, so they did not live in correspondence with him; their spirits were dead and so they had lost their balance. Man today is no longer governed by his spirit and his rational soul. He is governed by lust and desire. You notice that the apostle says that lust can apply not only to the body but also to the mind: 'the desires of the flesh and of the mind'. Did you know that the whole world is as it is today because of lust and desire? Man sets himself up as an autonomous, independent unit. He does not recognise God or his laws. He lives as he wants to and says, 'These are my rights. Why should I not express myself, why should I not have what I want?' But the trouble is that everybody else is saying the same thing. And so you get jealousy and envy and malice and spite and hatred, and you get rivalries and tensions and quarrels, and eventually you get wars between nations, the world divided into two, the haves and the have-nots, this side of the curtain, that side of the curtain, all out for the same thing. It is all the result of the fact that man has fallen from God and he is now behaving, not like an animal, but worse. Man is more devilish than any animal has ever been or ever will be. Man is more fiendish, he has lost his balance. The body is in control – all the lust, the passions, the desires – and man even glories in it. And in this way he is crucifying and destroying that which is highest in him, which is his rational soul and his spirit.

And so this world is a world of trial, and of shame. It is a world of disappointment, it is a world of unhappiness. And this is the only explanation for it.

Then I ask my next question – and these are all involved in a logical sequence. 'Very well, I see,' says somebody, 'you have told us now why the world is as it is; I want to know one thing more. What is the destiny of man?' And this is a tremendous question. Is man only an animal, and is it therefore true that when he dies that is the end – no point in life, death the end? If you take that view, you see, then I suppose that in many ways the logical deduction to draw from it all, if life has gone against you, is that it is best to get out of it! Commit suicide! Why go on enduring it? Why 'take up arms against a sea of troubles, and by opposing end them'? – if you can? Is it worth it? Is it worth the fight, is it worth the heartache? And many great philosophers in the dim past, in the time of the ancient Greeks, and many since then did go out by means of suicide, and it is very logical. But you see, death is not the end! Man has got this imperishable soul within him. The apostle says here, 'I know whom I have believed, and am persuaded that he is able to keep that which I have committed unto him against that day.'

When Paul says 'that day' he is referring to the end of the world, the end of history; this is God's final judgment of all men. The apostle lives in terms of his soul, and life and death, and 'that day', that which lies beyond. And this is the biblical view everywhere – that man is not just an animal, but a living soul, that death is not the end, that 'it is appointed unto men once to die, but after this the judgment', and beyond the judgment an eternity. But the soul does not end. And there are just two possibilities with regard to that eternity: either indescribable bliss and happiness and joy, or else indescribable misery and despair and an eternity of useless remorse.

My dear friends, these are the things that determine how you view life in this world; that decide how you live it and how you go through with it. Do you know you have got a soul? Do you know that that soul is imperishable, that it will have to stand before God and give an account of the deeds done in the body? This is the teaching of the New Testament. Our Lord taught it, 'This night thy soul shall be required of thee' – required of thee by God! And can you not see that these things, of necessity, determine how a man lives? If I have got a soul, then I do not live for eating and drinking and sex, and the so-called pleasures of the world. I do not stop thinking and say, 'Let us eat, drink, and be merry, for tomorrow we die!' I say, 'That is not the end, I go on. I am accountable, I am a responsible being, I must stand before my maker and give an account of my stewardship of the powers and faculties he has given me. How do I answer him?' And my whole life is determined and changed by my point of view with regard to these matters.

And so I leave a last thought with you at this point. What comfort is there and what hope is there for man in the light of these things? We find ourselves in this troubled world, so what can we do? That is a question we must ask. And let me answer that question dogmatically by saying that the biblical teaching is that man himself can do nothing about it, and that all his efforts will ever prove to be a disappointment. You may say, 'But this is pure pessimism! I am going out to make the world a better place, I am going to start agitating and we must put an end to war.' People have tried that before; they have tried everything. The whole story of civilisation is the story of the effort of man to put his world right. Man has always been seeking for that elusive happiness that he never finds. He cannot find peace. Let us not despise the great record of history and of civilisation. It has been a noble and a wonderful one. The striving of man, the intellect, the thought, the endeavour, all he has tried to do politically and in every other respect. But where has it brought us? Is it not about time that we drew up a balance sheet?

Why do man's efforts always end in failure? Why have all the great civilisations always come to nothing? Why is it that even non-Christian scientists are ready at the present time to predict that this is probably the last period in the history of the world and civilisation? What has gone wrong? Why do all our efforts come to nothing? What is this fatal something that dogs all the highest endeavours of man and brings them to a final futility? What is it? Does it not at any rate tell us that it does not lie in man himself to save himself? He has done his utmost and it has been a failure – magnificent but a failure nonetheless. It is not in 'man that breathes' to do it, neither is it in the so-called great world religions; every one of them is hopeless. Study them for yourself, they are all hopeless; the only hope they give you is to die out of this world and to be absorbed into some ultimate, some absolute in the end, some Nirvana. Man's individuality is lost in some of them. Man's only hope is in a series of reincarnations, says another; and so on you go. 'Look back to the past', says Confucius, 'worship your forefathers. It is the past that is great, let us try and get back to it.' There they are, these religions, all in their utter and profound hopelessness and despair.

But why is this? They are all finally hopeless because they cannot deal with this central contradiction that is in man. All

man's problems arise ultimately from that which is true of him
in the words of Jeremiah: 'The heart is deceitful above all
things, and desperately wicked: who can know it?' A man
himself cannot. He is on his own side. He can always make
himself appear better than he is. He can criticise another and
defend himself on the same point. Man is not honest. He
knows that he is a biased witness and that he is a fool. Look
again at Jeremiah's question: 'who can know the heart of man?'

And the answer is that there is only one who knows it:
'Thou, Lord, "triest the heart", and "triest the reins"'. So we
come back to this fact, that in the words of the apostle Paul,
what a man needs is to be *saved*. 'Who hath saved us', he says,
'and called us with an holy calling' (2 Tim. 1:9). Man needs to
be saved. He will never have peace and rest, he will never be
able to say, as he faces life at its worst, 'nevertheless I am not
ashamed' until he has been delivered from himself, delivered
from the thraldom of circumstances, from the world, the
flesh, the devil, delivered by God, to God, for God, and finds
his rest and peace in the arms of God.

And how does that happen? It is all here: 'I know whom I
have believed'. The apostle talks about 'our Lord and Saviour
Jesus Christ, who hath abolished death, and hath brought life
and immortality to light . . .' There is the answer. It all comes
back to that. There is no hope for man until, realising the
truth about himself and his final impotence and incom-
petence, he cries out unto the Lord just where he is. And the
Lord will hear him. The Lord who came from heaven and
lived and died and rose again – he will hear his cry. He has
said, 'Him that cometh unto me I will in no wise cast out.' He
stands and he cries to the world today in its tragedy and
shame, in its misery and failure, 'Come unto me all ye that
labour and are heavy laden, and I will given you rest.' He
says, 'I am come that they might have life, and that they might
have it more abundantly.' And when you have had that life
from him, even as you face death, you will be able to say with
this mighty apostle, 'To me to live is Christ, and to die is gain',
because it means 'to be with Christ; which is far better' (Phil.
1:21 and 23).

> 'Man may trouble and perplex me
> 'Twill but drive me to thy breast.'

That is the answer! 'Safe' – as the old hymn puts it – 'Safe in the arms of Jesus'.

Well, I hope to go on to tell you in greater detail about the Lord Jesus Christ. This is the only hope my friends – that God has not abandoned the world, that 'God so loved the world' – and rebellious, sinful, self-centred man – 'God so loved the world, that he gave his only begotten son, that whosoever believeth in him should not perish but have everlasting life', and that we on our part be enabled to say, whatever happens to us, 'nevertheless I am not ashamed: for I know whom I have believed, and am persuaded that he is able to keep that which I have committed unto him until [against] that day.'

Chapter Five

SUNDAY EVENING SERMON
10th May 1964

Christ our Saviour

For the which cause I also suffer these things: nevertheless I am not ashamed: for I know whom I have believed, and am persuaded that he is able to keep that which I have committed unto him against that day (2 Tim. 1:12).

We have seen that the only answer to the hopeless condition of mankind is salvation. We can do nothing for ourselves, but God has saved us. And Paul's whole case is that he is able to live as he is living and to react as he is doing even to prison and the possibility of death, simply and solely because he believes the gospel.

It is a gospel for every type of person and for all times and there is only one gospel. The apostle says in writing to the Galatians, 'Though we, or an angel from heaven, preach any other gospel unto you than that which we have preached unto you, let him be accursed.' Here (and again I would remind you to keep the whole passage, vv.6–14, in mind) he exhorts Timothy, 'Hold fast the form of sound words, which thou hast heard of me, in faith and love which is in Christ Jesus.' In the next chapter in verse eight he says, 'Remember that Jesus Christ of the seed of David was raised from the dead according to my gospel.' 'My gospel.' And when he says 'my gospel' he means the only one.

The other apostles preached exactly the same gospel. Paul is at pains to say that to the Galatians and to the Corinthians. There was no quarrel amongst the apostles. Peter went astray for a moment but he came back when Paul was able to remind him that he was departing from the common faith. There is a common salvation, a common faith, 'the faith once and for ever delivered to the saints,' and if it has been once and for ever delivered, what on earth does it matter that this happens to be the twentieth century? This is a revelation from God. This is not human reason, this is not man making discoveries. God, as the apostle says here, has revealed this. He 'hath saved us, and called us with an holy calling, not according to our works, but according to his own purpose and grace, which was given us in Christ Jesus before the world began, but is now made manifest . . .' That is it! And it has been made manifest once and for ever.

There is only one gospel. How long is this world going to last? I do not know. If it lasts a thousand years there will be no new gospel, there will be no need of one. This idea that modern man needs a new message is a denial of the whole of the gospel. Modern man! Who is he? Is he so much better than all who have gone before him? Is he more moral? Does he never commit adultery? Does he not commit fornication? Does he never get drunk? Is he not mad enough to build atomic bombs? Is modern man so marvellous that he needs a new message? Does he?

The problem is still how to live, how to die, how to face God in the judgment, how to contemplate eternity. That is the problem still, and the gospel still has the same answer. So thank God there need be no uncertainty about it. I know nothing in my preaching apart from what I find here. The apostle says to Timothy, 'Hold fast the form of sound words,' and these are the only words that I have, the very thing that he expounds in this paragraph. But the point that I would emphasise again is that you will only know the comfort and consolation, the strength and the power, of this message if you believe it as a whole. You cannot get any of the benefits of Christianity without believing the doctrines of the Christian faith.

Now there is another modern fallacy. I remember a man who had been a local preacher when he was young and making his career, but had since become famous. He was no longer a local preacher. One day he was questioned about his religion. 'Ah well,' he said, 'I still hold on to the Christian ethic; but of course I don't believe the doctrines any longer.' He did not believe the doctrines, he had become too wise for that, he had become a great man. 'But I still hold on to the Christian ethic.' There is only one answer to that. No man can practise the Christian ethic unless he believes the Christian doctrine and has the power that results from believing that. It is impossible.

The modern world is as it is because our foolish forefathers, about the middle of the last century, began to think that one could hold on to all the benefits of Christianity but at the same time deny its doctrines. Science had begun to make its voice heard in 1859 – Darwin's *Origin of Species* and all that accompanied it – and people said, 'Well, of course, we cannot any longer believe in miracles, or in the Virgin Birth, or in the miracles performed by Christ and things like that. Of course we cannot with all the knowledge we now possess, but we still want the benefits of Christianity.' And this twentieth century of ours is proving that we cannot have the benefits of Christianity if we shed its doctrines. We would like to, but it is impossible, because all the benefits come out of the doctrines. The life is the result of the belief. These two things are inextricably bound together and we can never divorce them.

Now, the apostle is saying all that here; he says he is 'persuaded', and that is why he is not ashamed. 'I am as I am,' he says, 'because I am persuaded of the truth of what I believe.' It is therefore essential that we should believe the truth. We will never know the experience until we do. Of course I do not deny that we can have false experiences. There are many agencies that can give them to us. I have known even Christian Science give people a temporary happiness. I have never known it help anybody to die, but I have known it make people happy for the time being, and many another cult can do the same thing. And, indeed, drugs can do it, and so can alcohol. Many things can give us temporary happiness.

But we are not interested in temporary happiness, we are interested in life and death and eternity, and this is the only thing that can really help us here; and therefore we must believe the doctrine. That is what Paul is exhorting Timothy to do. He says, 'You are as you are, Timothy, because you are not clear about your doctrine. You are evidently thinking that it all depends upon me, Paul; but it does not – it depends on the power of God. Do not look at me, get back to your doctrine, get back to your foundation. You will not be right, you will not succeed until you are clear about the truth.' I have to say exactly the same thing in this our day.

Now, we have seen that if we are to be clear about the Truth, we must start not with our own problems, but with God – God who created the world and controls it and has a purpose for it. Then, as we considered man, we saw that he is not just an animal. He is a living soul, made in the likeness of God, for God, for communion with God and for eternity.

But it is obvious that man is in trouble, and we have seen that he is so because of the devil, the god of this world, the evil power that persuaded him to rebel against God. Man is a slave of sin and evil and of the devil; and here he is, he is over-powered, he is over-mastered, he cannot fight them, though he has been trying to. The whole story of civilisation is the struggle of man against evil and against the devil. I am not here to detract from the glory of the achievement. A man who speaks against Greek philosophy or poetry is a fool. It was a noble attempt, but it failed. Consider these great civilisations; go and visit Athens, what will you see? You will see the glory that was Greece; not that *is* but that *was*. They have all come to the same end. They have never succeeded, indeed, they cannot succeed. All the reasoning and thinking, the philosophy and civilisation cannot solve the problem of man, neither, as we have seen, can the world religions.

Well then, is there no hope? There is indeed, and this is the whole point of preaching the gospel. I had to spend that time on the negative for this reason – that I know that no man has ever come to Christ until he has had to. I did not come to Christ till I had to. We are all so proud, self-satisfied, self-confident. We think we can do everything, and it is only when we are miserable failures and cast in the dust – 'I lay in dust, life's glory dead' – it is only then that 'From the ground there blossoms red, life that shall endless be' – this blessed hope for us. So when we see our utter hopelessness and helplessness and despair, we are ready to listen to the message of this gospel. What is it? Well here it is, the very thing that Paul is reminding Timothy about. And the thing that we want to look at now is that it all starts and centres in one person. 'I am not ashamed.' Why? Because 'I know [him] whom I have believed'. You see, Paul cannot leave him alone, he keeps on talking about him. In verse nine he says, 'Who hath saved us, and called us with an holy calling, not according to our works, but according to his own purpose and grace, which was given us in Christ Jesus before the world began, but is now made manifest by the appearing of our Saviour Jesus Christ'. Jesus Christ! Him 'whom I have believed'! It is always the same person.

Let me put it to you like this, quite simply. What was it that made this man, the apostle Paul the man he was? How could he be so happy there in that prison? How could he smile in the face of death? How could he rejoice in tribulations, as he was doing? You know there is only one answer – he had met a person! He had met this blessed 'him'. Before he met him Paul was Saul of Tarsus – a self-satisfied, complacent Jew, and yet miserable and unhappy. A self-righteous man is never really happy because he is always watching, he always has to be careful. If we try to save ourselves by living a life of morality and of religion we will never know happiness. Religion has never made anybody happy, neither has morality. It makes us decent, self-contained, but never happy. Morality has never made a man sing, neither has religion. They are all gloom. And that is why we must never lose the differentiation between religion and Christianity. It is Christianity alone that makes a man sing.

And what is it that made this man sing? Well, he tells us in many places, and we know his story. It was what happened to him on the road to Damascus. He went out 'breathing out threatenings and slaughter' against the Church, and then in the light from heaven, he saw that blessed face and heard a voice: 'Saul, Saul, why persecutest thou me?' and he realised that this was the Lord of glory! He met Jesus Christ! He got to know him! And his whole life was changed. He became a new man, living a new life, and here, in this passage, he is in prison and facing the end of it, but triumphing. Why? Oh, 'I know him; I know the one I met on the road to Damascus, and all is well with me because I know him'.

The whole of Christianity depends upon this blessed person. I wish that I did not need to keep bringing in these negatives, but I must. I have to give an account to God for my stewardship. 'We must all appear before the judgment seat of Christ', says this greatest of all preachers, 'and give an account of the deeds done in the body, "whether it be good or bad. Knowing therefore the terror of the Lord, we persuade men".' And in my feeble, unworthy way I must do the same thing. I know that we are living in a world which is telling men and women, as fast as it can and as frequently as it can, in books and articles and on the television and on the radio, that what matters is the teaching of Jesus, that Christianity means taking the teaching of Jesus and doing your best to put it into practice and to imitate him. But the apostle tells us here that that is a lie. 'Who hath saved us, and called us with an holy calling, *not* according to our works.' And therefore I have to say once more that it is not the teaching of the Lord Jesus Christ that matters to us primarily, but the 'person himself: *whom* I have believed'. The apostle is not saying, 'I am happy in prison because ever since I heard his teaching I have been doing my best to put it into practice and I can look back across my record', . . . but rather, 'I know whom I have believed, and am persuaded that he is able to keep that which I have committed unto him . . .' It is 'he'. It is all 'he'.

And, my dear friends, it is still the same today. I am not here to exhort you to practise the Sermon on the Mount, or to tell you to follow Christ. That follows, that comes, but I am here primarily to ask you a question: Do you know him? Have you met this Lord Jesus Christ? Is your confidence in Him?

Can you say, 'I know him whom I have believed, and I am absolutely certain that he is able to keep that which I have committed unto him against that day'? Therefore what I want to do now is again to hold him before you. And this is what the apostle reminds Timothy to do.

Let me remind you again that though Timothy was a preacher and an evangelist, yet the apostle had to tell him the elements of the Christian faith, and take him back to the very foundation principles. I am going to do the same, and I do not apologise for doing so. I am more and more convinced that all our troubles in Church and State today are due to the fact that we have forgotten first principles. People are assuming that they know what Christianity is, and they do not. They would not be what they are if they knew. This is Christianity. It is this person, and it is the facts about him.

What, then, are these facts? The apostle puts them before us. We start with 'Jesus'; 'Christ Jesus'; or 'Jesus Christ'. The apostle is as he is because he has met a person and this person's name is Jesus – Jesus of Nazareth. That is a man. That is the one who was born as a little babe in Bethlehem and whose body was cradled in a manger. They called his name Jesus. So we are looking at a man, and we must be clear about this, because our whole position is based upon this person who is a man called Jesus. But now here is the vital question: is he only a man? Is he only the greatest religious teacher and the greatest moral exemplar that the world has ever known – is that all?

Look at what the apostle tells us about him: 'But is now made manifest', he says, 'by the *appearing* of our Saviour Jesus Christ'. Whoever this is, he is one of whom we can say that he has appeared. Do you say that about ordinary human beings, that they have made an 'appearance' in this world? When a baby is born in your family, do you say, 'This child has made his appearance'? Of course you do not, you say he has been born – and you are right. But here is one who has 'appeared'! Epiphany! And what that means is that he existed before he appeared, he was there behind the veil, as it were, but suddenly the curtain was drawn back and he appeared.

Now, this is a part of the essential teaching of Christianity. We must, then, link that up with this other phrase, 'who hath saved us, and called us with an holy calling, not according to our works, but according to his own purpose and grace' – that is referring to God the father – 'which was given us in Christ Jesus before the world began, but is now made manifest by the appearing . . .' Now this is essential Christianity, and again it tells us not only that this is God's world but that he is still concerned about it and still interested in it. But, still more important, it tells us that even before the very foundation of the world God had conceived a great purpose and plan of saving this world. You see this is the thing the world does not know about. We are hanging on the lips of statesmen and politicians wondering what great philosophers are going to say, trying, as civilisation has always done, to get things a little bit better. But what you need to know is that God has a plan and a purpose for this world, and that the plan was there before the very foundation of the world. It was there in the mind of God, and has now been made manifest by the appearing of this person, Jesus Christ.

This is the message of the whole of the New Testament; indeed it is the message of the Old Testament as well, the whole of which looks forward to something, to the fulfilment of the promise that God made to fallen man in the Garden of Eden. When man fell God said to him, 'As the result of this, your punishment will be that there shall be perpetual enmity and warfare between the seed of that serpent and your seed, but the seed of the woman shall bruise the serpent's head.' There is to be a conquest over evil and sin and the devil and hell, and God is going to do it.

So, the whole of the Old Testament is looking forward to the fulfilment of this promise. That is the marvellous thing about the Old Testament. Once you begin to look at it with a New Testament eye you will see this unfolding purpose going on and on and on. God repeats the promise. God then takes a man called Abram out of paganism and turns him into one of his own men, and says, 'I am going to make a nation out of you,' and proceeds to do so. God does so because out of this man is going to come the seed of the woman that is going to bruise the serpent's head. There is the same promise. God said to Abram, 'Come out, count the stars if you can, count the sand on the seashore, such shall be your progeny.' 'In thee, and in thy seed, shall all the nations of the world be blessed.' The people of the Old Testament waited for this: and on and on the promise goes.

Indeed, it is repeated almost endlessly in the Old Testament. Come to Moses, the great lawgiver, the man who delivered the people out of the bondage and the captivity of Egypt and took them into the land of Canaan. Read how God instructed him about the furnishing of the tabernacle and how he told him what sacrifices to offer – blood must be offered, sacrifices have to be presented to God. Why? Because this is foreshadowing what God is going to do. A lamb has to be killed morning and evening, and so the ritual and the ceremony go on, repeated and elaborated in the Temple.

And as you read the book of Psalms, and as you read the messages of the prophets, you find the same thing. One of the greatest of all those prophets, Isaiah (the evangelical prophet as he is sometimes called), came to the people and he said, 'Comfort ye, comfort ye my people, saith your God'. Why? Because this great one is coming! 'Every valley shall be exalted, and every mountain and hill shall be made low . . . the rough places [shall be made] plain.' 'Prepare . . . a highway for our God.' 'The glory of the Lord shall be revealed, and all flesh shall see it together' (Isa. 40). 'Comfort ye'! He is coming! And that was the message of all the prophets. They were all looking forward to the coming of this mighty deliverer. Man is in the slavery of sin and Satan; he is helpless, he cannot do anything; he cannot keep the law; he is a failure. But the deliverer is coming, and the prophets are looking forward to him.

And then we come to this tremendous statement in the New Testament: 'When the fulness of the time was come, God sent forth his son, made of a woman, made under the law, to redeem them that were under the law' (Gal. 4:4–5). Notice the terms: 'when the fulness of the time was come . . .' God's purpose was there before the foundation of the world, before the world began. It was his purpose, his plan. And all till then had been preparation, but now the time had come: 'the fulness of the time'. The time was complete and he came. 'God sent forth his son, made of a woman, made under the law, to redeem them that were under the law.'

This is the great thing, you see! The 'appearing'! '. . . the appearing of our Saviour Jesus Christ'. That babe in the manger there in Bethlehem is none other than the son of God, the eternal son of God. 'In the beginning was the Word, and the Word was with God, and the Word was God . . . All things were made by him; and without him was not any thing made that was made.' The Eternal Word of God! But this is the message – 'the Word was made flesh, and dwelt among us' (John 1:1,3,14). The babe in Bethlehem is 'the Word made flesh'. He is the eternal son of God 'appearing'! He has entered into time, he has come into the world, he has taken on him human nature. He has become incarnate, he has added manhood to the godhead! Here is the whole mystery – the 'appearing'.

So you can know nothing about the Christian comfort and consolation until you believe in the virgin birth. Jesus of Nazareth is not just a man, he is not even perfect man, he is God-Man! 'Born of a virgin, conceived of the Holy Ghost.' Here is the faith of Paul, here is the faith of the early Church, here is the faith of the Church throughout the running centuries. Modern man cannot believe that. Well, then, modern man chooses hell! That is all I have got to say to him. It takes God as well as man to save man. And when you and I know the plague of our own souls, and when we realise the spiritual character of the law of God and our own moral and spiritual impotence, we will have no trouble about believing in the virgin birth.

Even the first man, Adam, who was made perfect in the image and likeness of God, sinned and fell; and God could not save the world by making another perfect man. The perfect man had failed. Not only can fallen man not save himself, perfect man cannot stand against the devil by himself. He

needs more, and more has come: 'appearing'! God the son
has come out of heaven into earth. 'God so loved the world,
that he gave his only-begotten son.' It is the seed of the
woman. He has no earthly human father. He is 'conceived of
the Holy Ghost'. Here is the one who had been prophesied;
the long-expected Jesus; the one of whom a message was
given to Zacharias, the father of John the Baptist; here is the
one of whom the archangel Gabriel spoke, when he came
to his mother, Mary, and said: 'Hail, thou that art highly
favoured, the Lord is with thee: blessed art thou among
women.' Mary was fearful. 'And the angel said unto her, fear
not, Mary: for thou hast found favour with God. And,
behold, thou shalt conceive in thy womb, and bring forth a
son, and shalt call his name Jesus. He shall be great, and shall
be called the son of the Highest: and the Lord God shall give
unto him the throne of his father David: and he shall reign
over the house of Jacob for ever; and of his kingdom there
shall be no end. Then said Mary unto the angel, how shall this
be, seeing I know not a man? And the angel answered and
said unto her, The Holy Ghost shall come upon thee, and the
power of the Highest shall overshadow thee: therefore also
that holy thing which shall be born of thee . . .'

This is not a mere man, this is God in the flesh! Here is a
person with two natures in the one person. He is perfect God,
he is perfect man. He has appeared! This is the central
message of Christianity. What you and I need is not a greater
message, or a greater teaching; we need someone who is
strong enough to deliver us and who can redeem us and save
us. And here he is – he has 'appeared'. God from the
heavens! Very God of very God! Son of God in glory! He has
come! '. . . the appearing of our Saviour, Jesus Christ'.

And then keep your eyes on him. The apostle, here in our
passage, is really giving a summary of it all. Look at this
person – 'I am what I am', says Paul, 'because I have met
him, because I know him, because I know that he is going to
keep that which I have committed unto him.' Well, very well,
let us look at him! Here is the one on whom everything
depends, He has been born as a babe, and laid in a manger.

But follow his story and listen to his teaching. He never went to the school of the Pharisees, he was brought up as a carpenter. And yet when he begins to teach, this is what people say about him: 'This man speaketh with authority, and not as the Pharisees and Scribes'. The soldiers sent to arrest him came back and said, '"Never man spake like this man." We could not touch him!' they said. 'There was something about him, there was an authority. We have never heard anything like it – "Never man spake like this man."'

Listen to what he himself has to say. 'Ye have heard that it was said by them of old time . . . But I say unto you.' 'I am the way, the truth, and the life: no man cometh unto the father, but by me.' 'Before Abraham was, I am'. 'I am come . . .' It is always the same. Not 'I was born,' but 'I am come'. He is the one who has come into the world; he is the fulfilment of the prophecy: 'The sun of righteousness shall arise with healing in his wings'. 'I am come,' he says. Notice his claims. He turns to men following their ordinary occupation and does not hesitate to say to them, 'Follow me'! And they do. Who is this who demands this kind of total allegiance, this surrender? Who is this man who puts himself apart and says, 'I am'? Who is this? Here is the vital question.

But look at the evidence again, look at his miracles. They are an essential part of the message concerning him. John, in his gospel, tells us that miracles were signs, that the Lord worked his miracles in order to give people knowledge as to who he was, and he used them as an argument when people did not believe him. He said, 'though ye believe not me, believe the works.' When poor John the Baptist, as the result of his imprisonment and ill health, had become troubled about Jesus and sent two messengers to him asking, 'Art thou he that should come or seek we for another?', he said, 'Go and show John again those things which ye do hear and see: the blind receive their sight, and the lame walk, the lepers are cleansed, and the deaf hear, the dead are raised up,' – and, here it is! – 'and the poor have the gospel preached to them' (Matt. 11:4–5). He worked miracles and people were astonished; they said, 'We are seeing strange things today. What is this?' They were filled with fear, and even his own disciples were alarmed. Miracles! Who, then, is this?

And then observe his perfect, sinless life. He was in the wilderness, tempted by the devil for forty days, but he did not sin; and he was able to say at the end of his life, 'Who can bring a charge against me?' And they could not. They failed. They tried to. But they completely failed. Here is one who conquers the devil, conquers evil, conquers all temptations. But then we discover something that seems to be a contradiction of everything that has gone before. We see this person, who can command the waves and cause them to be still, and silence the howling gale, who can 'make the lame man leap as an hart' and give life even to the dead, we see him arrested in apparent weakness, condemned and nailed to a tree, and dying the most shameful, ignominious death that it was possible for a man ever to die. There he is, dying in weakness, and we hear the shouting and the raucous laughter, and the jubilation of all his enemies. They have killed him; they have got rid of him. It is, they think, the end of him. They take down his body and they bury it in a grave. They roll a stone over it and seal it up. They put soldiers to guard the grave – and that is the end of Jesus of Nazareth.

But it is not! And this is the thing that the apostle reminds Timothy of here most particularly: '. . . is now made manifest by the appearing of our Saviour Jesus Christ, who hath abolished death, and hath brought life and immortality to light through the gospel' – this message concerning him and what he has done. He rises triumphant o'er the grave.

Now, my friend, the whole of Paul's case depends upon this. Read the early chapters of the book of the Acts of the Apostles and you will find that what they preached was 'Jesus and the resurrection'. Why the resurrection? Because it is the resurrection that finally proves who he was. Even the disciples were shaky until the resurrection. It was the resurrection that finally convinced them, and Paul says that he was 'declared to be the son of God with power, according to the spirit of holiness, by the resurrection from the dead'. If he had not done this he would not be the Saviour. 'He hath abolished death.' He has disannulled it, he has put it out of court, he has disintegrated it; and, at the same time, he has brought life and immortality to light – life and incorruption, through his gospel. Now, here, is the Christian message. It is found equally clearly in the sermon that Paul preached in Antioch of Pisidia found in Acts 13:16–41. It is a perfect exposition of these verses in Timothy. This is what Paul preached about this Jesus whom they took and put in a grave. But God raised him! And what does all this mean?

Let me just give you a summary at this point. God willing we shall go on to elaborate this more and more in detail, but it is all here – a perfect summary of Christian doctrine. It is the man who believes this, and who is sure of it, who is going to live and die as Paul did; here is the meaning of it all. It tells us who he is. It tells us that he is the son of God. David, as Paul argues in his sermon in Antioch of Pisidia, was a very great and wonderful man; yet when he died, his body saw corruption. But here is the only one who died and whose body did not see corruption. Here is one who has come out from among the dead, the first-born from among the dead, the first to rise: Who is he? He is God the son! That is what it proves. Everything about him proves it: his coming, his virgin birth, his 'appearing', his whole character, his life, his teaching, his miracles, his resurrection – they all prove the same thing, that this is none other than the son of God.

And what was he doing in this world? Well, we are told that 'God so loved the world, that he gave his only begotten son, that whosoever believeth in him should not perish, but have everlasting life.' He himself said that 'The son of man is come to seek and to save that which is lost'. He has not come to tell us how to save ourselves, he has come himself to save us. And he has had to come all the way from the glory to earth, and to go to the cross, and to be buried and to rise from the grave – he has had to do all this in order to save us.

So what has he done? To start with, he has shown us, what man is meant to be. He came into this very world that you and I are in – 'He came unto his own' – and he had the same problems and the same trials as we do. He 'was tempted in all points like as we are, yet without sin'. He did not live in some great pomp in a great house or in a palace or in a castle. No, he lived a life of poverty, the ordinary life of men and women, and was buffeted and battered. He saw the vileness and the evil and the sin of the world with his own eyes, at close quarters. He went through it all. But he has shown us how man is meant to live, he has shown us how a man can walk through it all and not be touched by it, not be tarnished by it, and not be polluted by it in any sense at all. When we look at him we see a perfect man, perfect manhood, man walking in communion with God through this world as man was meant to do from the beginning. We see it all there in him.

But, thank God, it does not stop at that! If that were all, he would be our greatest condemnation today. If there is one thing that is more fatuous than anything else it is this notion that we are meant to imitate Jesus Christ. For if you cannot satisfy yourself, how can you imitate him? The thing is monstrous, it is impossible. He is God, as well as man! Sinless! Pure! Perfect! And that is not all. For, why did he come? Well, it was not merely to let us know what man was meant to be; he came in order to conquer our enemies. Why do we fail in life? We do so because of our weakness, because of the power of the devil. Why does a man sin? It is because of the power of temptation and evil. Why is man afraid of death? We are all afraid of death by nature. We may pretend we are not; we sometimes whistle like children to keep up our courage in the dark. But the whole of mankind is 'subject to bondage', the fear of death.

Now, the reason for that, the apostle Paul tells the Corinthians, is that 'The sting of death is sin'. That is the trouble about death, it is sin. If there was not such a thing as sin, we would not be afraid of death. But there is sin, and man has a feeling within him that death is not the end, and that he goes on to meet God in judgment. He knows he is guilty, so he is afraid. Even though he has not much knowledge of theology, instinctively he is afraid. 'The sting of death is sin; and the strength of sin is the law of God.' We are conscious of unworthiness and condemnation, those are our enemies.

Christ has come to conquer every one of them – and thank God he has done so! As I have told you, he lived a sinless life; evil and sin could not touch him. What about the devil? Well, as I have told you, the devil had him for forty days in the wilderness and there he tried him, he plied him with his questions, and tried to catch him and to trip him – 'If Thou be the son of God, give a manifestation.' But Christ replied, 'Get thee behind me Satan.' He also said, 'Thou shalt not tempt the Lord thy God'; and so he dealt with the devil in that way by quoting scripture to him. He conquered sin and evil, he conquered temptation, he conquered the devil.

But the last enemy is death, with his terrible scythe; and every hour we live we come that hour nearer to him. He is there and he defeats all men. The stoutest goes down and so does the greatest. Can you not see them decaying? Great men entering into a kind of nonage again, a second childhood. They, like all men, are going to die. The last enemy gets everybody down. And before a man can live happily in this world, before he can live a triumphant life and be more than conqueror, he must not only be able to conquer the devil and sin and temptation, he must also be able to conquer death, he must be able to look through it, and to smile at the face of death; he must see beyond it, and there is only one way he can do that. This person! What has *he* done?

The Authorised Version is not as good as it ought to be in this passage. The tenth verse should really be translated like this: 'But now is made manifest by the appearing of our Saviour Jesus Christ, who on the one hand hath disannulled death' – disintegrated death, taken death apart – 'and on the other hand hath brought life and incorruption to light . . .' That is what he has done. He has conquered the last enemy. He has gone through death, and taken the sting out of it. He has established that death is not the end. He can turn to death and say, 'O death, where is thy sting? O grave, where is thy victory?' He has disannulled death. So even the last enemy has been conquered.

And on the other hand, he has brought life and immortality to light. The resurrection of Jesus Christ is an absolute proof that death is not the end. This is not the only life, nor is it the only world. There is another realm, another life, there is another world, which is incorruptible. There is no tarnish there. It is pure, it is immortal, it is glorious, it is absolute, and he has given us a glimpse of it. So that, knowing him and knowing the truth about him, I know that this is not the only life and the only world. I know that should man put me to death it is not the end. Indeed I know in Christ Jesus what the apostle Paul knew – that to me to live is Christ, and that to die is gain. It means being with Christ, which is far better. He has gone through death. He is the other side, he has gone beyond the veil and is in the glory: and I shall be with him. That is the faith of the apostle. 'I am not ashamed', he said, 'because I know whom I have believed, and I know that he has conquered sin, he has conquered the devil and hell, he has conquered the grave. He has conquered everything and my soul is in his safe keeping. And he who has conquered all my enemies will bring me to himself in the Glory everlasting.'

And at the same time, Paul knew that Christ, in his perfect life of obedience to God, had dealt with the other enemy, and that is the law of God: 'The sting of death is sin; and the strength of sin is the law', God's holy nature, his abhorrence of sin. How can I be just with God? The law condemns me. How can I keep the law? I cannot. Here is one who has. He has kept the law perfectly for me; '. . . made of a woman, made under the law, that he might redeem them that are under the law'. And he has done it by his active, perfect life of obedience, and on the cross on Calvary's hill. He bore the punishment that the selfsame holy law of God metes upon my sin and transgression, my evil and my guilt. He has done everything. Everything that I need, he has done; everything that gets me down and defeats me, he has conquered, and he alone has. It took Christ, who was both God and man to do it, 'the appearing of our Saviour Jesus Christ'.

My dear friend, the only way to live life, the only way to die, is to know Jesus Christ, to believe in him. I know him in whom I have believed. I believe that he is very God and very man. I believe that he came from the glory of eternity and was born of the Virgin Mary. I believe he demonstrated and manifested his deity in his miracles of power. I believe that when he died on the cross, he was dying in order that I might be forgiven. I believe that he was smitten with the stripes that were meant for me and that I so richly deserve. I believe he made his soul an offering for sin. I believe that he did so in a perfect manner and that he has rendered a complete satisfaction to every demand of a holy God and of a holy law. I believe that he arose literally from the grave in the body – the same body, but one that was changed and glorified. I believe in the literal physical resurrection – I have no gospel apart from it, for I would not know that he had conquered death apart from this, neither would I know that he is the son of God apart from this. I believe in the literal physical resurrection, whatever modern science may say. I believe that he ascended into heaven in the sight of his assembled disciples ten days before the day of Pentecost at Jerusalem on Mount Olivet. I believe they saw him passing through the heavens. I believe that he sent the Holy Ghost on the day of Pentecost. I believe that he will come again to receive those of us who believe in him unto himself, to judge the whole world in righteousness and to set up his eternal kingdom. That is what I believe. I know him in whom I have believed.

> I rest my faith on him alone,
> Who died for my transgressions to atone.

I have handed my soul and its eternal welfare to him, and I am persuaded that he is able to keep that which I have committed unto him until that day.

My dear friends, do you know him? Do you believe in him? Do you believe this testimony concerning him? 'Do not be ashamed of me,' says the apostle, 'or of the testimony of our Lord.' Are you more concerned about the opinions of men than you are about the opinion of God and of his Son? Are you afraid of ridicule and laughter? They will say to you, 'Do you still believe that? Do you believe in the virgin birth? Do you believe two natures in one person? Do you really say that you believe in miracles?' What does it matter what they say! They cannot live, they cannot understand life, they do not understand themselves, they cannot die in peace and they are not ready for the judgment.

Chapter Six

SUNDAY EVENING SERMON
17th May 1964, Whitsunday

God's Unchanging Purpose

For the which cause I also suffer these things: nevertheless I am not ashamed: for I know whom I have believed, and am persuaded that he is able to keep that which I have committed unto him against that day (2 Tim. 1:12).

As we continue to look at this challenging assertion of the apostle in which he states his faith, let me remind you that in this passage (vv 6-14) Paul is reminding Timothy of the great purpose of God. And we have seen that there is a purpose to life, there is a purpose to the whole world and God is at the back of all. God made, God created, God sustains, God is the artificer, God is the controller, God started time, God will end time. And the purpose of God in three persons, Father, Son and Holy Spirit, is to save man. Here is the hope that sustains the apostle.

Now this great purpose 'was given us in Christ Jesus before the world began . . .' This is a great comfort to me. What a blessing it is to be able to look up unto God and see that before he even made the world he had a great purpose of redemption. It is very good for our self-importance to read about the purpose of God before the foundation of the world. We must not get so excited about our little day and our little problems. Look up, I say, and look to eternity, the blessed glorious God and his purpose. And it comes especially in Christ Jesus our Lord. It was there given us in him before the foundation of the world – 'but is now made manifest by the appearing of our

Saviour Jesus Christ'. Now, we have been dealing with the coming into the world of the son of God. Jesus is the son of God! Man – but God! who has conquered our every enemy, even death, and who on that glorious day will come again and triumph over all his enemies and introduce his eternal kingdom of glory.

But it does not stop at that; that is not all. The son has appeared and has done his work in this world, and he has made this purpose of God the father actual and real. And having done it all, he has gone back to heaven and is seated at the right hand of God in the glory everlasting. But that is not the end – there is something further. The question is, how does all this come to us? How did it come to the apostle or to Timothy? How does it come to anybody? This section answers that question perfectly. There is still one other big event that we must look at.

The point I am trying to stress and to underline is that the Christian Salvation is based upon history. This is a fundamental point, and so many at the present time go astray here. We are so accustomed to philosophy, to ideas, and to thoughts. We say that we want some saving idea, some thought on to which we can hitch ourselves . . . But that is not Christianity. Christianity is God putting his purpose into operation. It was given to Zacharias, the father of John the Baptist, to announce it. 'God hath visited and redeemed his people.' The Bible is the book of the acts of God, and all our salvation depends, not upon ideas, but on the actions which God has taken in this world of time. That is why we can be so sure of it. Ideas come and go, they are found to be wrong and new ones are needed. But here are historic events, and I have been reminding you of some of them – how God made the world, then the history of the Jews, and God's interventions: God bringing them out of one captivity, sending them into another, and again bringing them back, and so on; and how in the fulness of the time he sent forth his son, made of a woman, made under the law. And then we have the phenomenon, the fact of history, Jesus of Nazareth, son of God, and the resurrection. A fact! Not an idea, but a fact. That is why we are given those details about his resurrection appearances and the different people who saw him. The apostle Paul gives a list of them in 1 Corinthians 15; those certain chosen witnesses. All these things are facts.

That brings us to this next fact, and that is the day of Pentecost – that which we celebrate on Whitsunday. What is Whitsunday? Well, it is the anniversary of that tremendous event which took place at Jerusalem, which is recorded in Acts 2. The citizens of Jerusalem were amazed, 'These people are all Galilaeans', they said, 'but we are hearing them all speaking in our own languages "the wonderful works of God".' What are these wonderful works of God? They are the things I have just been telling you about, and now, here before us, is the day of Pentecost. What happened on that day? Here were these people, meeting in an upper room, as they had been doing for ten days, and they were praying as they had been praying, and waiting as they had been told to by the Lord. 'Suddenly there was a sound as of a mighty rushing wind' – followed by the marvellous things described in Acts 2. What is this? Oh, this is the coming of the Holy Ghost, the third person in the blessed Holy Trinity, upon the infant Church. He has come to further the purpose of God, this purpose planned before the world began. The Son comes and does his work, and the Spirit is sent to continue it. These are facts.

This great and mighty fact which I want to hold before you is as much a fact as the birth of Jesus; it is as much a fact as his death upon the cross; it is as much a fact as his glorious resurrection; it is as much a fact as his ascension. The coming of the Holy Ghost upon that company of people and the wonderful things that happened are phenomena, they are facts of history. They are the beginning of something absolutely new. And, of course, that was how the people reacted to them in Jerusalem and everywhere else; they were confronted by phenomena. Here were these men, these apostles, Peter and the others – What were they? Well, they were very ordinary men, they were ignorant and unlearned men. Peter was a fisherman; some of the others were fishermen too. They had never been trained, they were not men of brilliant understanding and philosophic insight; they were most ordinary men, ordinary workmen, and everybody knew them. But suddenly these men are seen with the company of disciples speaking unknown languages, speaking with authority and filled with a spirit of glory and of exultation, and the people came crowding around saying, 'What is this?' A phenomenon!

Now, this is a part of the great purpose of God – the change in these men and their preaching, and the power that was given to them to work miracles, to do astounding things. So that this message spread and people heard it and believed it, and they became members of the infant Christian Church. As the message spread, this man Paul, then known as Saul of Tarsus, heard about it. He did not like it and he opposed it, but he was miserable while he did so. Yet he came to preach it! Why? What is this? And here Paul reminds Timothy of what it is. What is the meaning of that which happened at Jerusalem on the day of Pentecost? What is the meaning of this descent of the Holy Ghost upon the Christian Church? I say there is only one answer. It is God's purpose being carried on. The Spirit has been sent to further the purpose, to apply it, to extend it, to see that it is continued and that it will go on working until it is finally complete. And it is because of this that the apostle is able to write as he does, and no man will ever have this view of life and of death and this triumphant type of living as a personal experience until he believes all these facts.

So, let us look at the meaning of Pentecost. I do not want to delay you at this point with purely doctrinal or theological considerations, and yet they are important. You see how important it is that the fact of what happened on the day of Pentecost is a fulfilment and a verification of the promises of God. God, in the Old Testament, had promised that he was going to pour forth his spirit. Peter tells them that in his sermon on the day of Pentecost at Jerusalem. But you see the significance? The whole of the Christian position depends upon this – the purpose of God! That purpose that was planned, before the foundation of the world.

So God, knowing the plan and the purpose, now and again let out, as it were, bits of information. He gave previews of what he was going to do and foretold his plan centuries before it happened. He foretold the coming of his son, and all was fulfilled. He also foretold the coming of the Spirit, and on the day of Pentecost that, too, was fulfilled. So, you see, I have a verification of the purpose of God. I can believe in the purpose of God more surely because I have not only known the word of God, but I have seen that word fulfilled by the fact that the Spirit came, and that men and women were astounded in Jerusalem on the day of Pentecost, and were amazed by this phenomenon. I see the whole growth of the Christian Church coming out of that, and I can only explain the Church in one way, that it is the purpose of God. If the Church were merely a human institution, or the Church of men, she would have ended long ago; but she is not – she is the purpose of God! And so the day of Pentecost is a verification of the promises of God, and that in turn is a proof of his purpose.

But there is something more that we should learn from Pentecost and that is that it is also a proof with regard to the person of our blessed Lord and Saviour Jesus Christ. He says he is the son of God. Is his claim true? As I have shown you, the resurrection is enough to prove that it is, but here is a further proof. He said to those crestfallen disciples, unhappy at the thought of his leaving them, 'Let not your heart be troubled, ye believe in God, believe also in me'. And then he went on to say, 'I will not leave you orphans – I will not leave you comfortless. "I will pray the father, and he shall give you another comforter, that he may abide with you for ever; even the spirit of truth . . ."' (John 14:16–17). He said also, 'It is expedient for you that I go away: for if I go not away, the comforter will not come unto you; but if I depart I will send him unto you.' He committed himself. He said in effect something like this: 'Now, I leave myself in your hands in this way. I am going to be crucified, I am going to be taken from you; but do not be unhappy. I am going, but you will not be left alone, I will send the Holy Spirit unto you.' And if the

Holy Spirit had not descended on the day of Pentecost we would have a right to say that Jesus Christ is not the son of God and that he is not the messiah. But the coming of the Holy Ghost proves it. He had promised and the promise was fulfilled. He is the son of God! 'I will send him: another comforter.' So, we have God the father, God the son, God the Holy Spirit, and each one verifies, as it were, the word of the other.

But the thing I want to emphasise most of all here is that the coming of the Holy Spirit is the absolute proof that God is going to carry on his work. The Holy Spirit has been sent into the Church, the Holy Spirit is in the Church; the Holy Spirit is the third Person in the blessed Holy Trinity, and he is going on with the work until it shall be completed. Here is our comfort and consolation. I read my newspapers, I listen to the television and the radio, I hear the news, I listen to the speeches of the statesmen, I see their conferences, their coming and going and their planning and what they are proposing to do about the world. All right, it has got to be done, but I do not pin my faith to that. I know it is going to let me down, as it has always done; the world is not better than it was, it is worse. But I look at the Holy Spirit in the Church and I see the purpose of God, and I see these great mountain peaks of history; then I know that it is true. God is fulfilling his word, he is carrying out his promise. The coming of the Holy Spirit is one of these 'wonderful works of God'.

And how does the Holy Spirit further this work, this purpose of God? The apostle puts it here in one word. How can I get this view of life? None of us have it by nature. We are all of us, instinctively, afraid of life, we are still more afraid of death – of that unknown eternity. How can I get this certainty and assurance? How can all this become living and real and vital to me? There is only one answer – It is the work of the Holy Spirit. What does he do? He 'calls' us. Read those verses again: 'Be not thou therefore ashamed of the testimony of our Lord, nor of me his prisoner: but be thou partaker of the afflictions of the Gospel according to the power of God; who hath saved us, and *called* us with an holy calling'. Here is our

answer. Have you noticed the words that were uttered by
Peter at the end of his sermon on the day of Pentecost? He
said, 'The promise is unto you, and to your children, and to all
that are afar off, even as many as the Lord our God shall call.'
'Call'! He has saved us, and he has called us with an holy
calling.

What this means is that all that God has planned and
purposed is applied to me and becomes relevant in my life,
enabling me to speak as the apostle Paul speaks. It is only the
man who has been called who can do this, it is God's way of
bringing us to see the truth of the message, the truth concerning his eternal purpose.

Let us look, then, at this work of the Holy Spirit and see
what he does. We have seen that he calls us and we need to be
called because of the place and the condition in which we are
by nature. Where is that? The Bible is full of answers to that
question. Let me give it you in perhaps its most succinct form
in a word by the apostle Peter. 'You', he said to the Christian
people who had come into the Church both from Judaism and
from Gentileism, 'Ye are a chosen generation, a royal priest-
hood, an holy nation, a peculiar people; that ye should shew
forth the praises of him who hath called you out of darkness
into his marvellous light.' He has called us *out of darkness*.

This is the most relevant and urgent matter today. Why are
men and women defeated by life and unhappy, why are they
afraid of tomorrow, why are they afraid of death, why is there
all this uncertainty? Why is it that so few can face life and
death and all things as the apostle did? The answer is that they
are 'in darkness'. He has 'called us out of darkness'. Let the
scripture itself expound what this means. We are all by nature
in darkness, and there is darkness in us. Life is as it is, and the
world is as it is today because all mankind is in darkness. We
are all born 'dead in trespasses and sins'. We are dead! That is
our whole trouble.

The Bible means by this that we are dead to the life of God.
Is your life today determined and controlled by the fact that
you believe in the purpose of God? Are the lives of the
majority of people controlled by this fact? Is there any

thought of God in them? Is their life based upon God? What foundation have they got to their lives? And the answer is that God does not enter at all into any of their calculations. They start with man, they end with man; they start with this world, they end with this world. They are dead – dead in trespasses and sins. They are living as if there were no God, no purpose, nothing beyond man. They do not know about God, they are spiritually dead. They do not know that they have a soul within them, they do not know anything of the spiritual realm. Pleasure – drink, gambling, sex, money, motorcars – that is life to them, and they have nothing beyond it. They do not know of any unseen spiritual realm; they do not know of any qualities that rise above mere human thinking; they do not know of supernatural influences. They cannot say even with Wordsworth, 'And I have felt a Presence that disturbs me with the joy of elevated thoughts.' No, they are purely materialistic: they are bound by this life and this world.

And the result of all this is that they are ignorant and quite thoughtless and heedless. Of course, they are worried that there may be a war, they are frightened by the bombs, and they are troubled when illness and accident and death come along. But these things are only temporary. They do not really cause them to sit down and ponder and meditate upon it all seriously and profoundly. These things do not make them think and say, 'Well, what is going to happen to me? What happens when I die, where do I go, what am I, where am I going, what am I meant for?' They do not face these things. And that is why men and women are the victims of circumstance and chance – the state of the stock-market, the weather, and odd fortuitous things that tend to happen to them. These are the things that determine and control their lives. They have no idea of eternity, of an ultimate destiny; they do not think about them. And this is because they are spiritually dead, they are in darkness, they are ignorant, they do not know these things. That was the state of the whole of paganism; it had not got any knowledge of God, it was ignorant, 'their foolish minds were darkened', says Paul.

And not only that, when they do hear of the things of God,

they regard them as utter foolishness. They say, 'Do you really mean to say that people still believe in God? Do you mean to say that in the mid-twentieth century people still believe that Jesus of Nazareth is the son of God? Do you mean to say that people still believe in sanctity? This is a great joke, this is really very funny, fancy believing . . . foolishness! Nonsense! The whole thing is long ago outmoded, utterly ridiculed. This is indeed incredible – that in a scientific age people should believe in hell and in eternal punishment and the wrath of God! Why,' they say, 'is it possible that anybody still . . . ?' Foolishness! And of course the tragedy is that they think that they are in that position, and regard all this as foolishness, because they are the twentieth-century people, and because of the great advances of science and of knowledge. They are so ignorant that they do not know that people were saying exactly the same things in the first century. The apostle Paul tells us in 1 Corinthians 2, 'The natural man receiveth not the things of the Spirit of God: for they are foolishness unto him: neither can he know them, because they are spiritually discerned.' They said it all twenty centuries ago. Indeed, I can take you further back. The psalmist tells us, 'The fool hath said in his heart, "There is no God".' Ignorance! Darkness!

So there is man by nature, and that is why life is such a problem, and when death comes, everything has gone, the foundation has been lost. By nature we are dependent upon things and people, and when they are lost, we have nothing left; and then comes the fact of death and we do not know what is happening or where we are going. Ignorance! Darkness! We need to be 'called' out of it. And it is a part of the blessed purpose of God to call us out of it. And as he sent his son into the world to work out a salvation whereby he could reconcile us unto himself, he has now sent his Spirit, in order that he might call us to a realisation of these things. And that is precisely what the Spirit began to do on the day of Pentecost. God not only provides a way of salvation for us, he brings us into it, he calls us out of darkness into his most marvellous light.

There is a perfect instance of how God does that in the second chapter of Acts. Look at this man Peter – Peter, the fisherman, Peter, the braggart, the boastful fellow who said to our Lord the night before he was crucified, 'Though everybody should desert you I will stand by you.' And then, when he stood in the court listening to the Lord's trial, and the servant girl recognised him, he said, 'I do not know him'! And he denied him twice more – with oaths. The cad! The coward! To save his skin he denied his greatest benefactor, his greatest friend, his lord and master. Peter! But here he was, on the day of Pentecost, standing up with boldness and preaching – and not merely saying things, but saying them with power, and such power that they had a tremendous effect upon the people who were listening to him. 'Three thousand were added to the Church.' That was the work of the Holy Spirit. It was not Peter but the Holy Spirit using Peter, it was the Holy Spirit taking hold of him and using him as a vehicle and a channel to call men and women out of darkness into God's marvellous light.

How does he do it? Well, this is the whole glory of it all, and that is why I can say these things with confidence. You may think that everything I have said hitherto is rubbish and nonsense and folly; but, there is the Spirit behind me and in me and through me that can open your eyes and bring this thing to you with such force that you will cry out as these men in Acts 2 did, 'Men and brethren, what shall we do?' The Spirit of God is a powerful Spirit. He can act upon the mind, he can enlighten it, he can open it, and give it understanding. He can give it an ability that it formerly lacked. He can change the natural man into a spiritual man who sees and understands what formerly he ridiculed.

And the way in which he does it is often like this. We may be listening to something that we have perhaps heard many and many a time, when a new thing suddenly takes place. We begin to pay attention to these things in a way we have never done before. He brings the truth to us powerfully. We begin to listen in a way we have never listened before. We begin to see some meaning coming into what was meaningless to us before. We begin to attend to these things as Lydia began to attend to the preaching of Paul at Philippi. But, still more important, we begin to have a personal concern. This is what the Holy Spirit does. A man can come and listen to the preaching of the gospel and he can listen as a sermon-taster. He can be interested in the man, in the preaching, in the words, in many another thing; he can be interested in the argument, or in the particular thoughts, but he is listening in a detached manner, as a spectator, or as a judge, as he might go to a theatre and watch a play with the same detachment. It has got nothing to do with him. It is a matter of interest to him because he may have that particular kind of taste, but it is nothing more. But when the Spirit comes a man begins to listen in a personal manner, he begins to get a personal concern. This is what the Spirit does. It makes these things living and real and practical and relevant to us.

And what the Spirit does is, to show us God and something of the glory of God. He begins to enlighten our darkness and to expose our ignorance. We find ourselves thinking, 'I have never really thought about God, I have argued about God, and delivered my opinions about him, but I have never really thought about God at all, or what he is. Is God the almighty creator? Is God "light, and in him is no darkness at all?" Is God holy and just and righteous? God!' We begin to think about God and to realise that God is more important than the whole cosmos. The Spirit alone can bring us to that.

Then he begins to show us our own sinfulness. He really makes us face ourselves. And no man knows anything about the work of the Holy Spirit in calling until he knows something about conviction of sin. Our Lord said that 'he will reprove the world of sin, and of righteousness, and of judgment.' And he does. We, all of us, have lived a life of self-defence, self-excuse, self-explanation; we think, 'I am not so bad after all; I am not a perfect saint, of course, but . . .', meaning, I'm all right, there's not much wrong with me; everybody else is wrong but I am all right. We have never faced ourselves. But once the Spirit begins to apply the truth we face ourselves and we see ourselves for what we really are. David, for example – the great king David! – saw Bathsheba and lusted after her, committed adultery with her and then had her husband murdered in order to cover his adultery and get her for his wife. And he was quite pleased with it all, it was very clever. And then the Spirit of God began to deal with David, conviction came in, and David soon began to see himself as he really was. He said, 'Behold, I was born in sin; and in sin did my mother conceive me.' I am rotten, I am vile, what I want is a clean heart. 'Create in me a clean heart, O God, and renew a right spirit within me.'

Then take the apostle Paul, the very man who is writing here to Timothy; this man, before his conversion, was one of the most self-satisfied men that the world has ever known; a religious man, a moral man, who felt he had kept the law of God and that nothing more was required of him, all was well. But then the Spirit began to call him and to deal with him, and this is what he said about himself: 'In me [that is to say, in my flesh] dwelleth no good thing'. 'O wretched man that I am! Who shall deliver me from the body of this death?' All my righteousness, he says, is but as 'dung', it is refuse, useless, it is filthy, foul. He hated it! He had seen the blackness of his own heart, the self-righteousness, the self-assurance, the false idea of righteousness, and here he saw his vileness, his impurity, and his rottenness. And that is how the Spirit of God calls us.

And then the Holy Spirit reveals to us the fact that we have all got to die, and after death the judgment, when we must stand before God and give an account of the life lived and the deeds done in the body. We see, too, the law of God, threatening to thunder down upon us. Because God is who he is, he says, 'Thou shalt love the Lord thy God with all thy heart, and all thy soul, and all thy mind, and all thy strength; thou shalt love thy neighbour as thyself', and we have not done it. Nobody has done it, and we are therefore guilty. We are vile, and we are impure. We cannot dwell with that burning light! We are lost, we are damned, the wrath of God is upon us. And if we die like that it means that we go on to an eternity like that – an eternity of misery and shame, a realisation of our unutterable folly, of our uncleanness, impurity, and vileness: we realise it. And then we realise that try as we will we cannot change ourselves. Have you ever tried it? Have you tried to live a good life? Have you ever tried to imitate Christ? Some of the greatest men of the centuries have tried and they have all had to agree in the end, and all are ready to say,

> Not the labours of my hands
> Can fulfil Thy law's demands;
> Could my zeal no respite know,
> Could my tears for ever flow,
> All for sin could not atone.

Do your utmost and it is useless! We are hopeless and helpless. And yet we are moving forward; every day brings us nearer to death and the judgment that lies beyond it. And here we are, we see ourselves and we realise that we have got to meet this holy God. What can I do? There is nothing that I can do. So I cry out in my terror and in my alarm, as these men did listening to Peter: 'Men and Brethren, what shall we do?'

It is the Holy Spirit that brings a man to that, and that is how he calls men and women out of darkness, into God's most marvellous light. He reveals to us the horror of the darkness, our hopelessness, and our helplessness. We see it, and we cry out, 'What shall I do?' Then the Spirit gives the answer. 'Repent, and be baptised every one of you, in the name of the Lord Jesus Christ for the remission of sins, and you shall receive the gift of the Holy Ghost.' He unfolds to us – he was sent to do it – the truth about the Lord Jesus Christ, his saviourhood, his deity, his death on the cross, his resurrection, the whole purpose of God's way of salvation in Christ Jesus. He reveals to us all that he has done and all that he is going to do.

And the moment we see that and believe it everything is changed. We are in the light, and no longer in darkness; we have a new view of ourselves, a new view of life, and a new view of death, because we now see it all in the light of God's great and eternal purpose. God the father sends the son. The son does his work and goes back to the father. The Spirit is sent and the Spirit is doing his work. And what is that? It is to open our eyes, to bring us to see ourselves for what we are, and our precarious position, and then to see the wonderful provision of God for us. 'Who hath saved us, and called us with an holy calling, not according to our works, but according to his own purpose and grace.' And we begin to see ourselves as pilgrims of eternity, as children of God, knowing that we are living in a sinful, condemned, damned world, knowing that there is no hope for this world.

There is no such thing as world reformation; it will never come. The Bible says 'No'! The world is to be judged. There will be a new world, 'new heavens and a new earth, wherein dwelleth righteousness', and all who believe this message concerning him will be waiting and ready for it and looking for it, and they will spend their eternity in it. 'Let the world deride or pity; I will glory in thy name'!

'I have committed unto him' – what? 'My soul and its keeping "against that day".' The great day of the appearing of the son of God to judge the world in righteousness, to destroy evil and all that belongs to it, and to set up his glorious kingdom. And it was because he was certain of these things that Paul, the old apostle lying there in the prison, with Nero's sword playing, as it were, above his head, was able to say, 'nevertheless I am not ashamed: for I know whom I have believed, and am persuaded that he is able to keep that which I have committed unto him against that day'.

My dear friend, this is the question, have you been called? 'Who hath . . . called us with an holy calling.' Have you been called out of darkness? What is your view of life at this moment? What are you basing your life on? How do you look at tomorrow, at next year, at the future? Have you faced death? Have you faced what lies beyond it? Where do you stand? Where are you in life at this very moment? Have you got an understanding? Are you ready for all eventualities? Can you face the very worst and say, ' "nevertheless I am not ashamed:" I know where I am, I know what is going to happen to me; I am not afraid of the present, I am not afraid of the future.'

The terrors of law and of God
With me can have nothing to do;
My Saviour's obedience and blood
Hide all my transgressions from view.

My name from the palms of his hands
Eternity cannot erase;
Impressed on his heart it remains,
In marks of indelible grace.
Yes, I to the end shall endure,
As sure as the earnest is given;
More happy, but not more secure,
The glorified spirits in heaven.

Why am I sure of all this? Because it is God's purpose, it is the assurance of his purpose.

Things future, nor things that are now,
Nor all things below or above,
Can make him his purpose forego,
Or sever my soul from his love.

A man is only able to speak and to live and to die like this because he knows the purpose of God, this sure purpose that nothing will ever make God forego, the purpose planned before the world, revealed in the coming, the birth of the Babe of Bethlehem, the man Jesus, his death, his resurrection and ascension, the descent of the Holy Ghost – the purpose of God. It is certain, it is sure, and the facts proclaim it. And the ultimate fact will be the coming again of the son of God to wind up history, to judge the world in righteousness, to receive his own unto himself, and to set up his everlasting kingdom of glory.

My dear friends, I plead with you, I ask you again this

question: have you been called? Have you ever before realised the meaning of the day of Pentecost? Is your life based on God the father, God the son, God the Holy Spirit? What does all I have been saying mean to you? Have you been reading with detachment, just wondering how long it was going to go on, and hoping it was going to end soon? Or have you been hanging on my words because you have felt this to be vital to your soul, and you want to take in every word of it? Have you felt that you dare not live, you dare not die unless you know? Do you know whom you have believed? Do you see the purpose of God in your life? Are you in his purpose? Is this the most vital thing in the whole world to you at this moment? If it is, then I am glad to tell you that the Holy Spirit has done his work, he has called you! Called you out of darkness into God's marvellous light.

But if these things are not everything, and more than everything to you now, then I tell you in the name of God you are still in the darkness. If the fact that the very son of God came out of heaven and the everlasting glory and lived the life of a humble man, a carpenter, in this world; if the fact that he was born as a baby in a stable in Bethlehem and was put into a manger and endured all that he endured; if it means nothing to you, if he has died on that cross and it means nothing to you, then there is only one explanation – you are in gross darkness, you are dead spiritually, and the wrath of God is upon you.

But listen! God has sent his Holy Spirit into this world, into the Church, that the world may be called out of that darkness into his marvellous light. Have you seen yourself as a lost soul; have you seen yourself for what you really are; have you seen yourself in the judgment of God; have you contemplated eternity? Listen to this Word of God. Let these facts of history speak to you. Cry out, 'Men and brethren, what shall I do?' And as you do so I reply in the words of Peter: 'Repent', acknowledge and confess it. Give up self-defence, stop all your cleverness, admit you know nothing, for we do not know anything about these things by nature – repent! Believe on the Lord Jesus Christ, accept this message like a little child, cast yourself upon it and upon him and his love, and leave yourself, leave your soul, your eternal future in his hands. And then you will be able to say with the apostle, '"I am not ashamed", whatever the world may do to me, "for I know him whom I have believed", and I am certain that "he is able to keep that which I have committed unto him against that day".'

O blessed Spirit of God, pour out! Give power to hear, unstop deaf ears, soften hard hearts, bend stubborn wills, do thine own glorious work, and glorify the name of Jesus Christ the son of God, Amen.

Chapter Seven

SUNDAY EVENING SERMON
24th May 1964

God's Way of Redemption

For the which cause I also suffer these things: nevertheless I am not ashamed: for I know whom I have believed, and am persuaded that he is able to keep that which I have committed unto him against that day (2 Tim. 1:12).

Now those words in verse twelve are our basic text, but you will remember that we are actually considering the entire passage in which this particular statement is included. I am calling attention to it because it does represent so clearly and so perfectly the message of the Christian faith to this world today. There is no more false understanding of the gospel and of the Christian message than the regarding of it as a kind of philosophic point of view, just an attitude; it is, on the other hand, the most practical thing in the world. It is a way of life and it comes offering us a deliverance, a release; it offers us a new way of life, a way of triumph and of joy, a way of salvation, and it is this which the apostle puts so perfectly in the words of our passage.

Paul wrote these words, let us remember, in prison and under the shadow of death. Yet he says to the anxious Timothy, '"I am not ashamed", I am not put out, I am not despondent,' and he gives his reason for his confidence. Now, that is what we are considering together. What is it that enables the apostle in this way to face life, death and anything that a capricious man might do to him? What is his secret? And I am calling your attention to his answer to those questions because this is the very word that is needed by modern man. Nothing is more important than this. How are we getting on in life? How are we living? How do we stand up to advancing age? How do we face illness, how do we face loss of money or of employment? How do we face bereavement and sorrow in the family? How do we face our own coming death? What of the future?

Now, these are the questions, this is life, and the vital question, I say, is this – are we able to face it all as this man faced it? Can we say, 'whatever may happen to us, whatever disaster may come across our path, I am not disturbed, I am not upset, I have not lost hope, it makes no difference to me; "I am not ashamed"'? That is the question – are we able to say that?

Now the offer of the Christian gospel is to enable us to do that. That is what it is about. I know the gospel has got much to say about many of the pressing problems of life, but to me the whole tragedy of modern man is that instead of starting with his own problems, he is always considering somebody else's problems. People have got hold of the notion that Christianity is nothing but some endless repetition of a particular view with regard to certain subjects, just a handful of subjects, like peace and war and bombs and South Africa and so on. But, my dear friend, let me point out to you, your first problem is: how are *you* getting on? How are you standing up to the world, the flesh, and the devil? How do you face the fact of death that is coming? These are the very questions with which the gospel deals so plainly and so clearly. The apostle is in the position he describes not because of his temperament or background, but for one reason only, and that is that he believes this Christian gospel.

And we have seen that we can know exactly what this gospel is, and that it can be defined. We are in an age that dislikes doctrine, theology and definitions, and people prefer to talk about some vague spirit. But that is a blank contradiction of what the apostle says. Paul reminds Timothy of what he taught him. He tells him here very clearly, 'Hold fast the form of sound words, which thou hast heard of me . . . That deposit that was given you, that message that was entrusted to you by the presbytery, keep by the Holy Ghost which is given to us.'

There is no difficulty about telling what the gospel is, and fortunately for us the apostle in this one paragraph gives us a perfect synopsis of it. Paul wants to help this young man Timothy, and his whole argument in a sense is this: 'Timothy, you know you are really in trouble simply because you have forgotten the gospel that you are sent out to preach.' So he has to remind him of the elements of the gospel. And that is what I am trying to do for you here. We are living in such an age of confusion that we need to be brought back constantly to fundamental principles. I would argue that the world is as it is today because in almost every respect it is departing from first principles. We have forgotten principles, we have become pragmatists and utilitarians and various other things. We call ourselves practical men; we are not interested, we say, in definitions, we are only practical men. And we are; we are such activists that we have lost all our moorings, we do not know where we are and we need to be brought back to the first principles. And thank God they are all here before us! The apostle reminds Timothy of exactly what it was that he himself had taught him and what he is supposed to teach others.

Furthermore, let me repeat – and I feel I must go on saying this – it is no use coming to the Christian Church to get a particular blessing and to imagine that you can get that without believing its gospel. We cannot! We may well get something. We may get an emotional or psychological experience, but that is not the blessing of the gospel, that is a counterfeit. According to this teaching, no man can know any one single blessing of salvation without believing the gospel, without believing the message. That is Paul's argument. And it is Timothy's failure to hold on to these things that accounts for his shakiness, his uncertainty, his spirit of fear, and his being filled with forebodings and alarm.

I must keep reminding you of the whole case as it were, because all these parts of the gospel make up a composite whole. That is the glory of the gospel, it is the perfect plan of

God. Let me summarise it like this for you. Here is a man in trouble. Here is a man who is defeated by life, who is on the verge of giving up and going out through a back door that should never be opened; here is somebody whose heart is breaking and who is utterly bewildered and frustrated and baffled. Now what has the gospel got to say to such a person? What it says may sound a little harsh to you at first, but bear with me while we see exactly how it works out. The gospel is not merely a general word of comfort. It is no part of the gospel just to tell people, 'It is all right, do not be too upset, it is soon going to be better. You know you will soon forget, time is a wonderful healer, things are never quite as bad as you think they are.' That is an utter travesty of the Christian gospel. I know, God have mercy upon us, that the Christian Church very often has done that, and I believe that many people are outside the Church today – intellectual and strong people – because they say, 'I don't want sob stuff'. I am a hundred per cent with you. I do not want sob stuff either, and I have none to offer you. That is not Christianity. Christianity is the biggest and the strongest thing in the world. It is a great intellectual system that leads to a vital experience. It is a great whole, and I am trying to put it before you.

So instead of saying to us in our trouble, 'Cheer up, it is going to be all right, you know,' the Bible handles the problem, as we have seen, by making us start with God and with his purpose for the world which he has created. We have seen, too, how the Bible answers the question of man, who he is and the nature of his problem; how he has fallen from God and needs to be saved. That is the biblical case and this is what the apostle Paul preaches, and he is reminding Timothy of it and telling him to hold on to it and to go on preaching it after he, Paul, has been put to death.

Here is the message of Christianity. Man needs to be saved. He needs to be saved first of all from the *guilt* of his sin. Man is guilty before God. He has offended against him; he has broken God's laws and he is under the wrath of God. God does not bless the world as it is. He grants us certain blessings in spite of what we are. As our Lord said, '. . . he maketh his sun to rise on the evil and on the good, and sendeth rain on the just and on the unjust' – all alike. Thank God for that. The world would have been at an end long ago if God did not do that.

But what I am saying is that though God in his grace still gives us food and clothing and health and many other things, we are not living as man was meant to live, and this world is not as God originally made it and as God intended it. This is a travesty! This is almost the exact opposite of what God intended for man. It is not life as God meant it to be. All this is the result of man's guilt, man's punishment. God told man when he put him on probation, 'You go on obeying me and my laws and I will bless you; if you do not I will punish you.' God told man that, but man disobeyed and God has punished him. And, therefore, we need to be saved from the guilt of our sins, because we have sinned against God.

But, secondly, not only do we need to be saved from the guilt of sin, we need equally to be saved from the *power* of sin. We are all by nature under the power of sin. We prefer to do something that we are told not to do, and there is always some special charm about illicit fruit. The power of sin – who can stand against it?

Not only do we need to be saved from the guilt of sin, and the power of sin, we also need, thirdly, to be saved from the *pollution* of sin. The terrible thing about man is not simply that he does things he should not do, it is this nature of his that ever makes him want to do them; it is the element in man that responds to the attraction and the gaudy advertisement that is there before him. It is this pollution! Man is polluted in his mind, in his sensibilities; he is polluted through and through. Man is corrupt, he is unclean. And he needs to be saved, according to this message, from sin in that threefold manner.

Above all, of course, he needs to be restored to the favour of God and to the blessing of God.

Here, then, is the whole question; if our troubles are due to the fact that we are under the wrath of God and are not being blessed by God, the great question for us all is, 'How can I be restored to the favour of God, how can I get right with God?'

That is the supreme question. It is the one great question put in the Bible from beginning to end – 'How can a man be just with God?' Old Job put it, in his trouble, with that awful skin disease that was nearly driving him mad, 'How can a man be just with God?' It is the fundamental question. There is no hope of happiness and peace, and of real triumph and victory in life, until we are right with God and under his blessing. Oh, how can a man be just and right with God? Here is the crux of the whole question of salvation. How can a man be saved? How can I be saved from the guilt of my sin? How can I be saved from this awful power of sin? How can I be saved from this pollution that is in the very warp and woof of my nature?

See how the apostle deals with it. What a summary of the gospel we have here! 'Who hath saved us, and called us with an holy calling, *not according to our works . . .*' Oh, the importance of this negative! So much of the trouble today is due to the fact that people have never seen the meaning of it. We all tend to do this by nature. The moment a man becomes serious about life and begins to realise that he has got a soul – a soul which he had forgotten and had neglected completely and had done nothing at all about – the moment he comes to this realisation and sees that there is a God and that he has got to face him and give an account of himself and his life, his first and his instinctive reaction is almost invariably this: 'Now,' he says, 'I have suddenly seen it, I had forgotten all about this, I have been living as if I were an animal. But I see now that I am a man, I am a soul and I am dealing with God, and I need God's blessing. How can I get it? Very well,' he says, 'I must now start, I must turn over a new leaf, I must start living a new life, I must start reading the Bible, I must start praying; perhaps I had better give up my profession, I had better be a monk or a hermit or something like that, I must get into a monastery, for this is a whole-time job. I am going to live such a life that God will be pleased with it, and God will accept me, and God will begin to bless me.'

Is not that it? Is not that our instinctive reaction? Is not that the common impression as to what it is to be a Christian? Ask yourselves the question – what is your view of what it is that makes a man a Christian? What is a Christian? And I think you will find that by nature you have all at one time or another held this view: a Christian is a good man. A man makes himself a Christian by living a good life. A Christian is a man who is out to do good; he tries not to do evil and he does as much good as he can. That is a Christian.

And of course you have been encouraged in that false view by much of the teaching in the Christian Church. The Roman Catholic Church really teaches that. I know that it says the Church saves you, but through its sacraments and so on – yet it does leave a part to you. It puts great emphasis upon your co-operation. It is a synergism. It ultimately throws it back to you.

The Roman Church is not the only church that teaches that, such teaching is very common at the present time. Indeed, it is the prevailing and popular notion of Christianity, is it not, that Christianity means the imitation of Christ. How wonderful it sounds! We get to our feet as it were and we make a great sacrifice and we follow Christ. People like this. It appeals to a man's sense of the heroic and of self-sacrifice, and men who do this are regarded as the greatest Christians of the century, because they have given up so much and have done this and that. They are the great Christians, they are imitating Christ and living the life that he lived. That, they say, is what makes a man a Christian. It is a man's effort, self-effort, his works, his activities – these are the things that make a man a Christian.

And then others put it more in terms of what is called mysticism; in the end it comes to much the same thing. But it is a system that leaves it all to you; you have got to spend hours in contemplation and meditation; you have got to die to yourself, you have got to pass through the dark night of the soul, and it needs tremendous reading; reading philosophical books, and books on mysticism and the mystic way, and it means a rigid and a stern discipline and self-denial until, at long last, after you have gone through these stages you 'arrive'. That is the teaching of mysticism in its essence. We need not go into these things in detail. I am simply trying to show you that, instinctively, human nature, once it begins to realise its need of God and his blessing, once it realises that it is sinful and needs to be saved, immediately sets out to save itself. 'What must I *do* to be saved?' it says, and it is ready to do anything.

There are great and notable illustrations of this very thing in the long history of the Christian Church. There is no better illustration than this very man Paul who is writing here to Timothy. Before Paul became a Christian as the result of his meeting the risen Lord on the road to Damascus, he was trying to justify himself before God by his works. He puts it so perfectly, in Philippians 3: 'Though I might also have confidence in the flesh. If any other man thinketh that he hath whereof he might trust in the flesh, I more: circumcised the eighth day, of the stock of Israel, of the tribe of Benjamin, an Hebrew of the Hebrews; as touching the law, a Pharisee; concerning zeal, persecuting the Church; touching the righteousness which is in the law, blameless.' You see, he was proud and self-satisfied; he was trusting to his own works and he was quite sure that God was very pleased with him. He was a moral, religious man, a zealous man in persecuting what he regarded as heresy and blasphemy, and by these good works he felt that he was putting himself right with God. That was Saul of Tarsus! But his eyes were opened and he says, 'But what things were gain to me, those I counted loss for Christ. Yea doubtless, and I count all things but loss for the excellency of the knowledge of Christ Jesus my Lord: for whom I have suffered the loss of all things, and do count them but dung, that I may win Christ, and be found in him, not having mine own righteousness, which is of the law, but . . . the righteousness which is of God by faith'. There is a great example.

But you see it is not the only one; come down the running centuries and stop at the sixteenth. Look at Martin Luther. He was an excellent young monk who had given up the profession of the law, for which he was intended, in order that he might live this religious and devout life, but his conscience worried him and he still felt that he was a sinner and that he was under condemnation, and he wanted to be free, he wanted forgiveness. How could he get it? 'I will go into my cell,' he said, 'I will fast, I will sweat, I will pray, I will give alms'; and he set out to do this. He thought he could save himself by being religious, by doing these things.

But let me give you another example. Take 24 May, 1738, when a very remarkable thing happened in the city of London. I am referring to what happened on that day to a man whose name was John Wesley. Here was a remarkable man, born the child of pious and godly parents, always brought up in a religious manner. He went to Oxford and did brilliantly in an academic sense, but he was not content with that. He, too, was troubled, he wanted peace with God, his conscience was troubling him and he felt he should do more. So he began to preach to the prisoners in Oxford jail, thereby bringing upon himself the sarcasm and the contumely of his contemporaries, his friends and all round and about him. But even that was not enough. He gave up his fellowship of his college and decided to go out as a missionary to America. He undertook the hazards of a voyage in those days – but what was he trying to do? Well, he was going to *do* things that would put him right with God and earn his forgiveness, and give him peace of soul. So out he set to give his all.

This has been the history of the great giants of the faith throughout the centuries. Indeed it is all summed up by a pregnant phrase in Romans 10:3, in which Paul said that the whole trouble with the Jews was just that – that they were 'going about to establish their own righteousness'. They would do anything to establish their own righteousness with God – the effort, the trial of it all! That is what man does instinctively.

But all that is dealt with once and for ever in the phrase that is used here by the apostle: 'Who hath saved us, and called us with an holy calling, *not according to our works*'. Why not? Why are we not saved by our works? Why could Saul of

Tarsus not save himself – or Luther, or John Wesley? Why have all these mighty men not been able to save themselves? The answer is the great message of the New Testament and it is this: when you and I have done everything we can do and more, it is not what God demands, it is not what God asks of us. We hear people say, 'As long as a man pays twenty shillings in the pound in a moral sense, as long as he does good and lives a good life and is a benefactor, and as long as he is opposed to bombs and things like that – well, then, he is a Christian and God forgives him and all is well.' But, the Bible says it is not. Why not? Because it is not what God demands! That is what the apostle calls 'your own righteousness'. But they 'going about to establish their own righteousness, have not submitted themselves unto the righteousness of God', he says.

Now, this is a very vital matter. When modern man claims, 'I say that as long as a man lives a good life all is going to be well,' then I ask him, 'Who told you that?' A man said to me recently, 'You know, I am one of these practical Christians; I am not interested in doctrines, I am a man who believes in practising Christianity' – and then he told me about the good he was doing. Poor man! The question for him was, 'Who told you, and on what authority are you saying that that is enough? You may think so, but the Bible says the exact opposite. You are relying on your own righteousness.'

This is what God demands: not that you and I should do good, but that 'thou shalt love the Lord thy God with all thy heart, and with all thy soul, and with all thy mind, and with all your strength; and then you will love your neighbour as yourself'. You can be doing a lot of good, you can be a great world benefactor, but if you do not love God with all your being you are not fulfilling God's demands. That is what God demands. It is there in the ten commandments and I have given you the summary of the ten commandments as it was spoken by the Lord Jesus Christ himself. Without this, you may do as many works as you can, it will not help you, it is not what God asks. God does not ask how big a subscription you may have given to that good cause, how much money you may have sacrificed, how much sleep, or how much energy. He does not ask you these things. He asks, 'Have you loved me with all your heart, and soul, and mind, and strength; and have you loved your neighbour as yourself? Have you, or have you not?' That is God's demand.

Not only that, our works at their very best are always imperfect, they are always incomplete. But God asks for absolute perfection. As the apostle put it in Romans 10:5: 'For Moses describeth the righteousness which is of the law, that the man which doeth those things shall live by them.' God gave man a law and he said, 'Keep that law and you will satisfy me.' But we have got to keep it in every single respect. James, who was a very practical man, put it like this: 'for whosoever shall keep the whole law, and yet offend in one point, he is guilty of all.' It is no use keeping 99.9 per cent of the law. God demands absolute perfection, because he is perfect himself. He made man perfect and he will be satisfied with nothing less than perfection because he is what he is.

Where are your works and mine, my friend? When you compare your goodness with that of some great saint you have read about, how do you feel? Do you still feel proud of what you have done? But even his goodness is useless in the sight of God. As Paul says, it is but 'dung' and refuse; or as Isaiah puts it, it is as 'filthy rags'.

But there is something still more terrible. You read the lives of the greatest and the best men that this world has ever known and they are unanimous in saying that the more they have tried to please God, the more unworthy they have discovered themselves to be. Set out on the imitation of Christ and you will see hell within yourself. It is all very well to talk about philanthropy and to take an objective view. If you really take up the religious life, if you really try to live it in a monastery, if you try discovering God and knowing him and pleasing him, with an utter absolute perfection of obedience, you will find that you are a mass of pollution. You will say with the apostle Paul, 'In me (that is, in my flesh) dwelleth no good thing'. The greatest and the best men of all the ages are agreed on this.

Not the labours of my hands
Can fulfil thy law's demands;
Could my zeal no respite know,
Could my tears for ever flow,
All for sin could not atone.

I cannot do it! The more I try, the more God's holiness stands before me and I am shrivelled into nothing. I am helpless, I am hopeless, I am vile. 'Not by works of righteousness which we have done.' Bring out your good deeds, bring out your best, bring out all your philanthropy, bring out all the goodness of the universe, put it under the light of God's searchlight and where is it and what is it? Dung, and refuse; it is polluted, fermenting, and foul. No, man cannot save himself; 'not by works of righteousness which we have done'.

Let me put it as plainly as I can. Are you relying on anything in yourself at this moment? If you are, you are not a Christian. Are you relying on the fact that you have been brought up in a Christian country? God have mercy upon you! If you still think this is a Christian country I am afraid we are not speaking the same language. Are you relying upon the fact that you were christened when you were a child, or that you were baptised when you were older – is that what you are relying on? Are you relying upon the fact that you are a member of a church and that your name is on a roll – is that it? God have mercy upon you! Anyone can do that, especially today, when there is no longer strictness in these matters. Are you relying upon the good you have done? Are you relying upon the fact that you have never got drunk, that you have never committed adultery, that you are not a murderer – are these the things on which you are relying? Then, I say, you are outside! I do not care how respectable you are, you are outside. 'Not by works of righteousness which we have done' – 'not according to our works'.

So, what is it? What is the essential thing? Well, the apostle tells us, and he introduces it with this blessed word – 'but'. 'Not according to our works, *but* according to his own purpose and grace, which was given us in Christ Jesus before the world

began, but is now made manifest by the appearing of our
Saviour Jesus Christ.' What is it? Oh, it is that which changes
everything; the thing that turned Saul of Tarsus into Paul, the
apostle; that turned the hopeless monk Luther into the
mighty Protestant reformer; this is the thing that happened to
John Wesley on the 24 May, 1738, in that little meeting in
Aldersgate Street. When he went in to that meeting, he was
broken-hearted, miserable, unhappy, ill in body, soul and
spirit, feeling utterly hopeless, but he came out a new man.
He had made the discovery of this 'but'. '. . . not according to
our works, but according to his own purpose and grace'. This
is the message: that it is God who saves us; that no man can
save himself, but that God in his great purpose and in his
grace has found a way to save us and to deliver us. God's
purpose, planned before the foundation of the world, and his
grace.

What does grace mean? It means favour to people who do
not deserve it at all. It is unmerited favour. That is grace! And
this is the blessed message of the Christian gospel today, that
as we are utterly and completely hopeless, it is God's grace
that saves us. We do not deserve it. Nobody deserves it. We
are all vile, we are all hopeless, we are all sinners, we are all
reprobates. But God has a purpose, and it is a purpose of
grace, and he has worked it out, we are told, 'in Christ Jesus
before the world began, but is now made manifest by the
appearing of our Saviour Jesus Christ, who hath abolished
death, and hath brought life and immortality to light through
the gospel'.

Here is the message – that a man can only be saved and
reconciled to God by Jesus Christ the son of God, and by what
he has done. The apostle Peter put it once and for ever in a
statement that he made when he was on trial before some
great authorities and powers: 'Neither is there salvation in
any other: for there is none other name under heaven given
among men, whereby we must be saved.' This is the only way.

Why is that so? Why cannot a man save himself? Why did it
necessitate the coming of the son of God out of heaven into
this world? Why was the incarnation essential? Why did not

God save us somehow or other by a mighty word? If he could create the world out of nothing, could he not give a saving word out of nothing? He could not! There was only one way whereby man could be saved. And the reason is that you and I are in this position of having broken the law of God, and God's law must be honoured. God's law demands a perfect obedience, because of the character of God who is holy, who is light and in whom is no darkness at all; so the law of God must be honoured and obeyed in every jot and tittle. It is a terrible thing to break it, for it is an insult to him, it is rebellion against him: the enormity of the thing! God's law must be honoured in every detail, in absolute perfection. That is one demand, but there is another.

What about the sins that we have committed? How are we going to deal with the guilt of sins committed? How are we going to erase this guilt? How are we going to get rid of all that is against us in the law of God? Our sins need to be expiated, and the honour of God needs to be propitiated. That is the demand. Man cannot be saved until his guilt is expiated, and until he renders a perfect obedience to God. But he cannot do it. 'Well, then,' you say, 'why did not God create another perfect man?' The answer is, you see, that the first man was perfect. It is no use creating another man because Adam was created absolutely perfect. There was no sin in Adam. He was entirely innocent and entirely free from sin. He was made in the image and likeness of God. He was given an original righteousness from God, he was a perfect creation. But the perfect man fell. He failed – the devil was too much for him. It was no use sending another man.

There is only one way whereby you and I could be saved, which was that someone who, at the same time, was both man and yet greater and bigger than man, should come to deliver us. Now the apostle puts this in a memorable phrase in Romans 8:3,4: 'For what the law could not do, in that it was weak through the flesh, God sending his own son in the likeness of sinful flesh, and for sin, condemned sin in the flesh: that the righteousness of the law might be fulfilled in us, who walk not after the flesh, but after the Spirit.'

Now there it is all in a nutshell and what it means, you see, is this: the giving of the law to man could never save us. Because it left it to man to carry it out and man has failed to do so. 'All have sinned, and come short of the glory of God.' 'There is none righteous; no, not one . . . all the world may become guilty before God.' Man cannot keep the law of God. He was given it, but he failed to keep it. 'What the law could not do'! So God in his infinite grace and kindness sent out his own son. The Baby of Bethlehem is the eternal son of God. God's purpose needs a perfect man, but more, a perfect God, and in him we have God and man, two natures in one person. Here is one bigger than man because he is God and man, and he is able to do what we have failed to do.

And he came into the world and he rendered a perfect obedience to God's holy law. God looked down upon him from heaven and said, 'This is my beloved son in whom I am well pleased.' He never disobeyed, he never rebelled, he never failed. He was without sin; 'in all points tempted like as we are, yet without sin'. We need a high priest, says the author of the epistle to the Hebrews, who is 'holy, harmless and undefiled, separate from sinners'. And here he is, alone. Here is the only one who as man has trodden the face of this earth and has given an absolutely perfect obedience to the law of God. It was God who sent him, and God sent him to do that. It is God's grace that sent him. 'God so loved the world, that he sent [he gave] his only begotten son . . .' He came and lived the law perfectly, and then he went obediently to the cross.

And what was happening there? Paul, in Romans 3, has answered the question: God set him forth as a propitiation for our sins. This is why Christ died on the cross on Calvary's hill. God took your guilt and mine and put it there on his son. The son was innocent, he had never sinned. But he made himself responsible for our sins. Read what Paul says in 2 Corinthians 5:19,21: 'God was in Christ, reconciling the world unto himself, not imputing their trespasses unto them . . . For he hath made him to be sin for us, who knew no sin; that we might be made the righteousness of God in him.' 'It is God "who has saved us,"' he says, '"and called us with an holy calling, not according to our works . . ." It is his purpose and grace.' And there it is carried out in Christ upon the cross. 'And the Lord hath laid on him the iniquity of us all.' 'Yet we did esteem him stricken, smitten of God, and afflicted.' He is 'the lamb of God that taketh away the sin of the world'.

All the Old Testament teaching had said that the lamb that was to be sacrificed should always be without blemish, it should be absolutely perfect. This prefigured the coming of the perfect son of God, perfect God and perfect man, on whom God laid the iniquity of us all. He has smitten him, and stricken him. He has punished him for my sins, and Christ has borne my guilt: 'Who his own self bare our sins in his own body on the tree; that we, being dead to sins, should live unto righteousness; by whose stripes ye were healed.'

My dear friend, that is the message of salvation. That is the way in which a man is saved. It is the only way to be forgiven, to 'believe on the Lord Jesus Christ'. That is the 'form of sound words'. 'This is a faithful saying, and worthy of all acceptation, that Christ Jesus came into the world to save sinners; of whom I am chief.' I cannot be blessed by God until I am reconciled, until my sin is forgiven and dealt with and expiated. I must be restored. And it is Christ who came and lived and died and rose again, sent of God, according to his purpose and grace, in order to do that for me. And all I am asked to do is to 'believe on the Lord Jesus Christ'. Not by works that we can do, but simply by coming in helplessness and hopelessness and despair and saying again with Augustus Toplady:

> Not the labours of my hands
> Can fulfil thy law's demands;
> Could my zeal no respite know,
> Could my tears for ever flow,
> All for sin could not atone;
> Thou must save, and thou alone.

So I go to him and say:

Nothing in my hand I bring;
Simply to thy cross I cling;
Naked come to thee for dress;
Helpless look to thee for grace;
Foul, I to the fountain fly;
Wash me Saviour, or I die.

This is the thing that enabled the great apostle to speak like this, and to say that though he is in prison and face to face with death, yet he is not ashamed, because he can say, 'I know whom I have believed'. 'I know that I am a child of God, I know my sins are forgiven, I know that God is my father, and I know that his promises are ever sure, and that he has said, "I will never leave thee, nor forsake thee" – "I will hold thee, I will maintain thee, I will be with thee". "I am not ashamed: for I know whom I have believed, and am persuaded that he is able to keep that which I have committed unto him against that day." Christ has saved me from ignorance. He has saved me from the wrath of God and from the tyranny of the world, the flesh and the devil. He has saved me from hell, he has saved me for a new life – the life of God in the soul beginning here and blossoming in the glory of eternity.'

My dear friends, I simply ask you the inevitable question – do you know whom you have believed? Do you realise that you cannot save yourself? 'Not by our works.' Do you ascribe all the praise and the glory and the honour to God, in his great and eternal purpose, in his wonderful grace in sending his only-begotten son, the Lord Jesus Christ, into this world to live, to die, to be buried and to rise again, that you might be forgiven, and be reconciled to God; so that you might become a child of God and an heir of everlasting bliss? That is the one essential which will enable you to say, whatever happens to you: 'I am not ashamed: whatever comes, I am ready. I know whom I have believed.'

Chapter Eight

SUNDAY EVENING SERMON
31st May 1964

Abundant Life

For the which cause I also suffer these things: nevertheless I am not ashamed: for I know whom I have believed, and am persuaded that he is able to keep that which I have committed unto him against that day (2 Tim. 1:12).

As we look once again at these words – and indeed at the whole passage – let me remind you that we are doing so because here, I say, we have the essential Christian message to this world in which we are living today. There is no more false view of Christianity than that which regards it as some kind of vague, nebulous idealism, just one amongst a number of philosophies, but something rather remote from life, something which is essentially not practical. That is the biggest mistake out. The whole Bible claims that it is what we may call the text-book of life. It is a book that is given to us in order to enable us to live. My contention is that there is no more practical book in the whole world today than just this very one into whose message we are looking together in this way and manner. How often have I put it like this, that the Bible tells us much more about life as it is today than the newspapers: much more. Because it deals with life at a more profound level. It is not merely interested in superficialities. It gives us a real insight into life, and it explains to us why everything that happens does happen. That is why the Bible is always contemporary. It is God's book about life, God's book about himself, about man, about life, death, eternity, and all these matters that are of such vital importance to us, every one.

And here, in these verses, the apostle gives us a perfect summary of this great and glorious gospel. I am filled with amazement every time I read this particular paragraph, because the apostle, as I have reminded you, was writing here to a preacher, and when a preacher becomes depressed there is only one reason for it, which is that he has forgotten his own gospel. Here is the apostle Paul having to remind this young preacher Timothy of what are after all the fundamental tenets of the Christian faith, because he knows that no man can overcome life and death and all things except the man who really believes the faith and who commits and submits himself to it.

Now, we have seen that our first need is the need to be saved, to be reconciled to God, and to receive again God's favour and compassion and clemency. And God has provided for this: '. . . not according to our works, but according to his own purpose and grace, which was given us in Christ Jesus before the world began.' So, then, our first great need is to be forgiven, to be restored to the favour of God. That is a fundamental message of the Christian faith – justification by faith only. We are saved by God, who sent his only-begotten son, 'that whosoever believeth in him should not perish, but have eternal life.' There is the first thing.

But it is not the only thing, and so many people stop at that point. They think that Christianity is just a message which offers people pardon and forgiveness, which tells them that God is ready to smile upon them and to be reconciled with them and leave them at that. There are many people who are interested in Christianity for that reason. They do not want to go to hell, they say, they do not want to suffer; so they believe in the forgiveness of sins. And that is the totality of their view of Christianity. But it is something which falls very far short of this full message of which the apostle reminds Timothy in this one section, without going any further.

What else does man need? Well, here is a very wonderful thing. Man ultimately needs life. And all his troubles, as I want to try to show you, are due to the fact that he really is not living, that he does not possess real life. And one of the most wonderful aspects of the Christian message, is that it is a message which offers us life! It does not merely forgive us and leave us where we were; that would not enable a man to overcome in this life – to overcome life and death and all things. No. Forgiveness, wonderful though it is, is only a means to an end. Forgiveness has got to come first. There are no dealings between God and man while man's sins are upon him. God does not bless the sinner. Before the sinner can be blessed he must be forgiven, he must be washed, he must be cleansed, he must be restored to communion and fellowship with God: so we must always put forgiveness first.

But it does not stop there. Man is forgiven in order that he might be given the gift of life. Now there is no point, perhaps, at which the modern misunderstanding of Christianity goes so hopelessly astray and away from the real truth as this one, where it fails to realise this blessed message which I am holding before you here. Life! Our Lord said, 'I am come that they might have life, and that they might have it more abundantly.' Why did he put it like that? He did so because man is lost. He described the human race since the fall, and in sin, 'as sheep without a shepherd'. That was his view of mankind – that man is like a lost sheep. And not only a lost sheep but one who, because he is lost, does not know where to find pasture, does not know where to get adequate and suitable food. Not only that, he is at the mercy of all the dogs and the wolves, and of all the marauders that are ever threatening to attack him and to take his very life from him. 'All we like sheep have gone astray', and the result is that man, according to the Bible everywhere, does not live, he merely exists.

Now that is obviously a very vital, and a fundamental matter. There is all the difference in the world between existing and living. This is a fundamental point, I say, because our whole view of life determines our ultimate attitude towards these questions. Let me give you a modern illustration, which shows it to you in a bold and almost rude manner.

Medical people have become so clever today that they can keep dying people alive in a most extraordinary way, and there are some people whom they have kept alive for months. How? They put them on a machine which keeps the heart pumping, and the lungs and the kidneys working, and the patient will exist like this until the machine is switched off. The person is still alive. But the question I ask is – is that person living? We can keep a person in a state of existence, but that is not living. This person is still there, we cannot say that he is dead while his heart is pumping. We cannot sign a death certificate. But I say that that person is not living but existing.

Now take this into the spiritual realm, and it is exactly what the Bible says about man in sin and man as the result of the fall. The Bible says that what men and women regard as life is not life at all, because if there is no fundamental and true understanding of life, it is not life, it is mere existence. If there is no object or real purpose in life, then, I say again, it is not life, it is nothing but existence. When a man lives, there is always an element of mastery and of control and of understanding. There is a fulness about it. But is it not painfully clear that men and women in the main today know nothing about that. Are they not just the victims of circumstances and of their surroundings and of their environment? That is the extraordinary contradiction in the life of the modern man who is always boasting of his superiority to all who lived before him. He boasts of this, and yet man has never been more of a slave than he is today. He is the 'mass' man. He is the result of advertising and of propaganda and of manipulation. There is no question about this. People are thinking less and less; their whole pattern of life and their whole idea of life and of living, is being determined for them by these tremendous agencies that have come into being. Man becomes more and more a machine, and more and more the result of the interplay upon him of all the various media, these powers that are controlling thought and outlook.

Work this out for yourselves. Is it real life and living when man does things without thinking as to why he does them? Is man as inventive as he was, is he as personal in his enjoyments as he used to be? He does not even play games nowadays. Everything is being done by somebody else, everybody is being manipulated, and the television programme for the day determines how a man is going to live. He looks at the programme and there it is. At this hour he does this – at that hour that . . . and so life is taken out of his hands and he becomes a machine; he is being worked by buttons that are being pressed by somebody else. I say that is not living, that is existence!

Now, the apostle Paul, long ago in the first century, put that in a famous phrase. He reminded the Ephesians that, before their conversion, that was the sort of life they had lived. He put it in these words: 'Wherein in time past ye walked according to the course of this world, according to the prince of the power of the air, the spirit that now worketh in the children of disobedience'. 'The course of this world'! the merry-go-round of life, man being manipulated by 'the thing to do'. I say that is not life, that is existence, the 'mass' man, the 'machine' man, the man who has lost his individuality and his own control over life. Is this not true? A man does not live when he is just a reaction to other people or to other things or to other ideas. A man is meant to be positive, he is meant to control. He is not to be a mere reaction to something that somebody else does, or something that is done to him.

So it is because of all these things that our blessed Lord uttered those words, 'I am come that they might have life, and that they might have it more abundantly.' He says that he has come to save the lost sheep. He has come that he may lead them in and out, and that they might find pasture. They are no longer to be like bedraggled sheep, constantly at the mercy of the attackers and not knowing where the green pastures are where they can feed and lie down and enjoy themselves and be made fat and flourishing. They must be delivered from where they are and be transferred into this new existence. That he tells us, is why he has come: 'that they might have life, and that they might have it more abundantly'.

What does this abundant life mean? How can we get it?

Have we got hold of the principle that Christianity offers a man a new life? This is what often makes people feel that Christianity is what they call a fairy-tale, the idea that by waving a magic wand a man can have a new start. But, you know, that is precisely what it does offer! It does not do it with a magic wand, but it does do it in its own way. How can I get this life? The answer to that question is quite plain. The apostle puts it for us in this very paragraph which we are considering together. Read again the qualifying phrase: 'not according to our works'. 'God', Paul says, 'hath not given us . . .' It is God who gives. It is according, not to our works, but to the God who gives.

Now this is again one of these very fundamental matters. Look at the way the old question puts the problem: 'Can the Ethiopian change his skin, or the leopard his spots?' 'Can that which is crooked be made straight?' Can a man change his own nature? Can a man suddenly transform himself into something essentially different? Well, every man who has ever tried to do it knows that the answer is no. A man cannot do it. But that is where this blessed message comes in. It tells us that the gospel is in this world and that Christ came into this world to do for us what we cannot do for ourselves. It is only because man is a failure that the son of God ever came. If man could do it, Christ would never have come, the ten commandments would have been enough. There is the way of life, and we are told, 'Live that life'. But a man cannot do so. He may want to with his mind but he will find there is something in him dragging him down, as Paul puts it in Romans 7.

So, how can I live this new life and where can I get it? I need life! And the answer is that it is God who gives it. 'I am come that they might have life, and that they might have it more abundantly.' 'The wages of sin is death; but the gift of God is eternal life through Jesus Christ his son (our Lord).' These are the great terms of the New Testament. The apostle says again in writing to the Ephesians, 'We are his workmanship, created in Christ Jesus . . . .'.

This is one of the most vital things that people must understand and grasp. It is the failure to grasp this that accounts for the rejection of the Christian message by so many people at the present time. They do not understand that it offers them life – that it is not merely a point of view or an ethical and moral code. It is these things, but it is much more; it enables us to live. You see, what man needs is not new teaching, it is new power. All the great philosophers throughout the centuries have been trying to give us teachings and they have been exhorting us; but that is not the fundamental need of man. Man's trouble is that though he knows what he ought to do, he cannot do it; he knows what he ought to be, but he is dragged down by his lusts. And the need of the human race today is not instruction, it is ability, it is power; and this is the very thing that is offered us by the gospel when it offers us this new life.

How does it give us this? Now, here is a great question and a very vital one; people have always stumbled at this. Let me summarise the teaching for you. It tells us that we are given this new life as the result of the operation of the Holy Spirit of God upon us. This is not man's work, it is God's work And the very terms which are used explain this in and of themselves. The Bible talks about a 'rebirth', about a 'new creation', it talks about 'regeneration', and these of necessity mean that it is the work of God himself, the creator at the beginning, offering to create again. He offers to give man a new start. This is essential Christianity, and it is only as we realise this that we shall be able to react to life and to death in exactly the same way as the great apostle did.

Let us, then, be clear about this mighty work. The very essence of the Christian message is that a man can have a new start, he can have a new life, he can have a new beginning, he can be made a new man. Now, that is the thing in which I glory, the thing that makes preaching so romantic, and always so hopeful. It enables me to say that I care not what a man's previous condition may be when he enters a service. He can be the biggest slave to sin that the world has ever known and it does not matter. The preacher, you see, is not exhorting people, he is not simply telling people to live a better life, or simply saying that they can be forgiven, and then stopping there, because that would leave them where they are. No, he is there to offer new life, 'life which is life indeed', life which is full, life which is whole, life which is new, and he is doing so because it is the work of the Spirit of God; it is not a man changing himself. Any teaching that says a man can change himself is a denial of the Christian gospel. It is God who changes people. He makes anew. And because of that, of course, it follows that this is a very mysterious work.

Let us look at the third chapter of John's Gospel in order that I may bring out this very point. Our Lord established it there, once and forever, in his conversation with Nicodemus. Here was this great Jew, this teacher of Israel, this man who had been listening to our Lord's preaching and teaching and had seen his miracles. He went to Jesus at night and said, 'Rabbi [Master], we know that thou art a teacher come from God: for no man can do these miracles that thou doest, except God be with him.' And there is no doubt that Nicodemus was on the verge of putting a number of questions, and one of them would almost certainly have been this: 'Tell me, how have you got this extra power? I am a master and a teacher of Israel, I am able to do things that the people do not do, but you have got more than I have. What is this extra something? I wish I could get it!' But our Lord interrupted him saying, 'Verily, verily, I say unto thee, except a man be born again, he cannot see the kingdom of God.' You see, he diagnosed Nicodemus, he saw what was happening in Nicodemus's mind. He saw that Nicodemus was saying to himself, 'I want this extra thing; what must I do in order that I may be like him?' And our Lord said, 'Nicodemus, stop! You are wrong, all wrong! You have got to be born again.' And Nicodemus could not understand this; fencing very cleverly he said, 'How can a man be born when he is old? Can he enter the second time into his mother's womb, and be born?' Poor Nicodemus! How ridiculous and foolish his cleverness became when he put it against the son of God! He thought he was scoring a brilliant point – 'How can a man be born when he is old?' What is the use of saying to an old man, 'You must be born again'? The thing is impossible! And our Lord's reply to him is this: 'That which is born of the flesh is flesh; and that which is born of the Spirit is spirit.' 'I am not talking about the flesh, Nicodemus,' he said, 'I did not say you could go back into your mother's womb. I am not talking about giving a man another start in a physical or a material way. I am talking about giving a man a new start in the spiritual realm.' Poor Nicodemus did not understand and our Lord looked at him and said, 'Marvel not that I said unto thee, ye must be born again. The wind bloweth where it listeth, and thou hearest the sound thereof, but canst not tell whence it cometh, and whither it goeth: so is every one that is born of the Spirit.' 'This,' says our Lord to this man, 'is a mystery and you are trying to understand it. Give up, give in, you never will. It is like the wind, you cannot see it, you know its effects, you can see the result, but you do not understand it; there is a mystery, it is God!'

So there, once and for ever, our Lord has established the principle that this new birth, this act of regeneration, is not only the work of the Holy Spirit, it is such a mystery that no man can ever understand it. People say, 'But you know life is not like that. In life I get what I work for. If I am a good student I will pass my exam, if I am diligent in my work I will get promotion or an increase in pay, and now you come and you say, "Do nothing, it is given to you, it is God."' Well it is because this is not man, but God. We are not talking in the realm of the flesh, but in the realm of the Spirit. It is God's work and it is a very mysterious work.

And it is also a very deep work, and thank God for that, because what is offered us by the Christian message is that we will be changed, not only on the surface but also in the very depth of our being. Christianity is not merely a superficial washing, not merely something that changes a man in his externals and turns a vile person into a respectable person. It does that, but it also does something much bigger, it changes a man's heart, it changes his very spirit, it changes him in the depth and fundamentals and vitals of his being.

Now the apostle put it in very plain language in 2 Corinthians 3:3 where he said, '. . . ye are manifestly declared to be the epistle of Christ . . . written not with ink, but with the Spirit of the living God; not in tables of stone, but in fleshy tables of the heart.' And there is the most perfect description of the difference between morality and Christianity that you will ever find. Morality is written on tables of stone. It is rules and regulations which say, 'Do this'; and that was the law given through Moses to mankind; but that is not Christianity. Christianity is a work which is done in the 'fleshy tables of the heart' – not outside a man but inside him. A man who becomes a Christian does not just become a conformist, he is made anew. He is changed in the depth of his personality. He has a new heart. Christianity is the answer to the cry of David in his psalm: 'Create in me a clean heart, O God; and renew a right spirit within me.' It is a fulfilment of the prophecy that was given through the prophet Ezekiel in the thirty-sixth chapter of his prophecy, where God said, '. . . and I will take away the stony heart out of your flesh, and give you an heart of flesh'. Man's heart is a stone and he needs one of flesh, and the new birth means the stony heart is taken away and the heart of flesh is put in its place. It is a deep and profound work, it is nothing less than a 'new creation'. It is a 'regeneration', it is the God who created at the beginning creating a new man and bringing into being something that was not there before.

Now that is the offer: a new life, which is life indeed. It tells us that a new principle can be put into our very constitution, that a new disposition can be given to us and that we will start a new life as new men.

Let me then ask a final question. What are the characteristics of this new life? You see, the apostle Paul is able to write like this about life and death because he is a 'new man in Christ Jesus'. That is his favourite expression. The Christian is a man who is 'in Christ'. When we look at that proud, self-satisfied Pharisee, Saul of Tarsus, and then look at the apostle Paul, we find it difficult to believe it is the same man. But it is the same man, absolutely changed: the same individual, the same birth date, the same everything; and yet new, absolutely new. A revolution has taken place.

What are the characteristics of this new life? Let me just give you some headings to think about. What this new birth really does is to make us 'children of God'. The apostle Peter says that we become 'partakers of the Divine Nature'. Now, if you and I could only grasp something of the meaning of that, we would be able to live and die as the apostle Paul did. It means that I become a child of God, adopted into the royal family of heaven. I am still a man but there is this new something about me, that I have been made a partaker, of the very Divine Nature, a child of God. In other words, God no longer looks at us in terms of law, but in terms of love. He becomes our father. He is interested in us and we can go to him, we have access into his very presence, though he is eternal and all-glorious and holy. We are 'children' of God.

And the moment a man realises that he is a child of God it changes everything. It changes his views and his outlook entirely and completely. When a man begins to understand things in this new way as the result of the new life that he has received, he gains an entirely new view of himself. What is man? I ask that question again in order that you may face it. Is man only an animal? Well, if you think you are an animal and nothing but an animal you will live accordingly and sooner or later you will be defeated by life. The moment you realise what man is, and that you are a child of God, you will have an absolutely new view of yourself, and because you have a new view of yourself you will have a new view of the whole of life.

The moment a man sees this, he sees that life is not an accident and that it is not something entirely contingent, without end, object or purpose; he sees that life is a tremendous thing and that he has got to go on to meet God. He sees himself as a child of God away from home, as it were, for a while, but being prepared for that which God has got for him; in other words he has got an entirely new view of life. And inevitably, therefore, he has an entirely new view of his own destiny. The apostle again sums it up in a great phrase: 'if any man be in Christ, he is a new creature; old things are passed away; behold, all things are become new' – and it is a literal fact. When a man becomes a Christian he never sees anything again as he saw it before.

Let me give you some illustrations of what I mean here. Listen to the psalmist breaking out one morning in a poem of praise and saying, 'The heavens declare the glory of God'. Do the heavens declare the glory of God to you? You see, when a man becomes a Christian and gets this new life and nature, when he becomes a 'partaker of the Divine Nature', he sees everything, the whole creation, in a different way. He looks at the heavens and he sees the glory of God. The sun, the moon, the stars, the thunder, the lightning, all these things are God's handiwork; and as he looks at nature and creation, he sees God and the marks and the imprints of God's fingers. Let me give you that in the words of a poet who put it in the form of a hymn beginning like this:

> Loved with everlasting love;
> Led by grace that love to know;
> Spirit, breathing from above,
> Thou hast taught me it is so.

Then he goes on:

> Heaven above is softer blue,
> Earth around is sweeter green;
> Something lives in every hue,
> Christless eyes have never seen:
> Birds with gladder songs o'erflow,
> Flowers with deeper beauties shine,
> Since I know, as now I know,
> I am his, and he is mine.

To the natural man, to the botanist, a flower is very wonderful, but it is nothing but a collection of petals and stamens. He can see the order and the arrangement, but no more. An atheistical scientist can discover many of the wonders of nature and creation but he cannot use that kind of language.

A primrose by a river's brim
A yellow primrose was to him,
And it was nothing more.

And that is one of the tragedies of life today, that so many people go to the country but do not see it. They sit there and litter it with their bottles and their refuse, but they do not see its glory, they do not see God, the marvel, the mystery, the wonder, the colour – God speaking, God blessing, the almighty God who fills the universe and who has brought everything into being. But the moment a man has this new life he has a new eye, a new eye for beauty, for symmetry and for order. 'Something lives in every hue, Christless eyes have never seen.'

But not only does he have a new view of everything, he is also imbued with new purposes and he has a new object in life. What is life? Why does one live? Why does one go on living? How are we going to spend this next week? What are we looking forward to? Is it just to do the job and to be paid, and to eat and drink and indulge in sex, to look at television and go to a cinema, or perhaps do this or that? Is that life? I say that is existence! There is no purpose there, no grand objective. But you see, the moment a man is born again and receives this new life, everything is changed. The apostle again argues like this: '. . . we thus judge, that if one died for all, then were all dead: And that he died for all, that they which live should not henceforth live unto themselves, but unto him which died for them, and rose again.'

So when a man becomes a Christian in a real sense, he does not live for himself, he lives for Christ, he lives for God. He is a pilgrim going to eternity and he sees the world as a kind of preparatory school. This is not all, this is not everything; it is a mere preparation for that glory that is coming, when God shall be all, and in all, when the great ultimate regeneration shall take place and 'Jesus shall reign where'er the sun doth his successive journeys run'. This man now lives to please God and to glorify him and to enjoy him for ever.

And finally, it is a new life which gives a man new desires.

Did you notice how Paul puts it: 'Who hath saved us, and called us with an holy calling'? When the Spirit of God deals with us he 'calls us out of darkness into his marvellous light'. This new life is a holy life. And Paul emphasises this, because it is very germane to his argument. What is it that makes life in this world what it is and as it is? There is only one answer: it is sin. Why are men and women unhappy? Why do some commit suicide? Why are most people heedless and thought-less and afraid to think, and especially afraid to think of death? The answer is that it is all due to sin. All unhappiness in this world, all the ultimate problems of life are due to sin. God made a perfect world, it was Paradise, there was no trouble, there were no problems and there was no unhappi-ness. And the great message of the Bible everywhere is that all the trouble in the world is the direct and immediate result of sin. There is a phrase in the Old Testament which sums it up, saying, 'The way of transgressors is hard'. And it is.

Let me show you what that means. Sin never satisfies – never! I need not stay to prove that, need I? We have all tried it, we have all sinned. Has sin ever really satisfied you? Sin never satisfies. And people who continue in sin become the victims of lusts; these drives, these passions, these impulses stronger than themselves; and the more a man sins the more he wants. There is a sense in which the poor drunkard's thirst can never be satisfied, and the lust of man and his craving can never be satisfied. And that is why sin always leads to trouble. Once a man breaks the law of God and does something that he should not, he does not get satisfaction, he has to go on from that; one divorce, for instance, may lead to another, and so, one sin leads to more and more and more. Of course, every time, sin says to you, 'Just do this once and you will put everything right.' But you do not, you go on to the next sin, and on and on and on; like the prodigal son's, it is a rake's progress and it goes from bad to worse. Why? Because sin never satisfies and it always leads to restlessness. 'The wicked', says Isaiah, 'are like the troubled sea when it cannot rest, whose waters cast up mire and dirt.' And the world is restless today because it is a world of sin.

And in the same way sin always produces misery. Whenever a man breaks these laws of God he always suffers remorse. I know he tries to brush it off, or to drink it off. He tries to get rid of it by sinning still more, but it comes back, it is still there. Remorse, misery, a sense of failure, and of unhappiness: the morning after the night before! Sin always does that. It leads to misery, to a sense of emptiness, a sense of uncleanness, a sense of vileness. In the same way, sin always produces loss. Whenever a man sins he always loses something. He loses his honesty, his chastity, his purity; he loses his idealism, he loses his nobility. Sin always robs, it takes from us. It disintegrates the personality and makes man a collection of mere impulses and desires; it makes him into a liar and a cheat. He has to cover himself up and he lives a double life, and all this leads to confusion and disintegration of the personality.

And, finally, sin always produces fear. This is a world that is filled with fear – the explanation of the modern pleasure mania is its fear. Men and women are running away from life, they are seeking an escape. It is not the gospel that takes men away from life, it is not religion that makes men escapists, but the lack of it. Look at the people today who, instead of facing life, are looking at thrilling, exciting things on television, which are no more than pure imagination; and when one item finishes they switch on the next without any thought, and on and on they go. That is escapism. And drink is also escapism, as are all these things, used because man is afraid.

And sin, of course, always leads to trouble with others. Read those terrifying, searing words that the apostle wrote to Titus: 'For we ourselves also were sometimes foolish, disobedient, deceived, serving divers lusts and pleasures, living in malice and envy, hateful, and hating one another.' Look at life behind the veneer today. Look at the life of the people of the smart set who are too clever and modern to be Christian. How affable they seem to be, how they love one another, there are no troubles there. But listen to them whispering; they speak through the corners of their mouths, and they sneer at one another, and they metaphorically cut one another's throats. They are 'hateful, and hating one another'! Why? It is because they are sinners, because their hearts are rotten, because they are vile and have lost the face of God.

When a man becomes a Christian, however, all that is changed. He has new desires, he is 'called with an holy calling' to a holy life. 'We were like those other people,' says Paul to Titus, 'sometime'. 'But thank God,' he continues, 'now things are different. – "But after that the kindness and love of God our Saviour toward man appeared, not by works of righteousness which we have done, but according to his mercy he saved us, by the washing of regeneration, and renewing of the Holy Ghost; Which he shed on us abundantly through Jesus Christ our Saviour: that being justified by his grace, we should be made heirs according to the hope of eternal life."' Thank God this gospel calls us, as Paul puts it in the previous chapter of Titus – 'Teaching us that, denying ungodliness and worldly lusts, we should live soberly, righteously, and godly, in this present world; looking for that blessed hope, and the glorious appearing of the great God and our Saviour Jesus Christ'.

My dear friends, this is the life that Paul was living, and it was *living*. It was a holy, godly life, no longer governed by lust and passion and desire; no longer hateful and hating, but the life of a new man created in the image of God and after the pattern of the son of God himself. This new man had been washed and renewed, he had been re-created. He was 'a new creature; old things are passed away; behold, all things are become new'. And when a man becomes a Christian he sees life differently and he sees death differently. Indeed, he sees everything differently, because he is now a child of God who knows that he is but passing through this evil world, and that another world is coming. Christ is going to bring a new heaven and a new earth wherein dwelleth righteousness. He knows that this is God's world and that God is not going to leave it like this. He knows that the devil is not going to have the last word, and that evil is not going to persist endlessly. He knows too that the son of God will come back, the very one who defeated Satan when he was here before, and who even conquered death, the last enemy and has brought life and

immortality to light. He knows that Christ will come back and
rout his every enemy and defeat his every foe, that evil and sin
will be banished, and that there will be a new heaven and a
new earth, where righteousness will dwell. Then, but not until
then, there shall be no more war. Men will no longer be
hateful, and hating one another. They will not then vie with
one another in killing and harming one another; they will all
be new creations, the sons of God, and their supreme delight
will be to know God's dictates and obey.

Now what the apostle is telling us is, that it was because he
not only believed these things, but had experienced them,
that he was able to face imprisonment and even his coming
death with utter, absolute equanimity. 'It is all right
Timothy,' he says, 'what are you getting excited about? Why
are you frightened, why are you ashamed of me and of the
gospel and toying with the thought of toning down your
message in order that this may not happen to you? Man alive,'
he says, 'hold fast! Remember what you are; remember that
you are a child of God, a pilgrim on the way to eternity, and
that what they do to you if they put you to death is simply to
usher you immediately into the presence of your blessed Lord
and master. "I am not ashamed: for I know whom I have
believed, and am persuaded that he is able to keep that which
I have committed unto him against that day".'

But, my friend, you will never be able to say that until you
have got new life, a new spirit, a new heart, a new mind; you
will have to see everything differently. You will see drink
differently, you will see politics and sex differently, in fact,
you will see everything differently – today, tomorrow,
yesterday, the future. Everything will be transfigured, you
will see all things with a new eye, and you will be able to say
with honesty, 'We have the mind of Christ, and we now see all
things even as he saw them.' He came from the glory into this
world, saw life at its worst, was tempted in all points like as we
are, yet without sin. He met his death triumphantly and
conquered it, and even the grave; he rose triumphant, and
returned to the glory everlasting. And I know that because I
belong to him, and my soul is in his safe keeping, I

likewise will arrive in the glory and shall see him and be with him for ever and for ever.

But you only get into this position when you believe the gospel, the fundamental tenets of the Christian faith, and as you believe them, you experience this new life with all these things to which it inevitably leads. I ask once more, do you know whom you have believed, and are you happily and confidently leaving yourself and all your circumstances in his blessed, beloved, all-powerful hands?

Chapter Nine

SUNDAY EVENING SERMON
7th June 1964

Delivered from Fear

For the which cause I also suffer these things: nevertheless I am not ashamed: for I know whom I have believed, and am persuaded that he is able to keep that which I have committed unto him against that day (2 Tim. 1:12).

The point at which we have arrived, in our dealing with this wonderful assertion of the apostle Paul, is that the Christian is not merely a man who is forgiven, he is changed – changed completely, he undergoes a rebirth, regeneration, new creation. These are the terms which are used about this tremendous thing that happens in a man who becomes a Christian. He becomes a new man with a new outlook, new desires, new hopes, new everything.

Now we take up this again, because I imagine somebody still has a question to put to me. 'All right then,' you say, 'I believe all that you have said, I accept that, but still, you know, a man has got to live in this world, and how can he live in a world like this?' You say, ' "Believe this, believe on the Lord Jesus Christ", and that is all right in a chapel, but then I go back into the world and it is exactly as it was before. How can I live when the world, the flesh, the devil, and all their powers are set against me – how can I live? Have you anything to say there? Has the gospel anything to say at that point?'

Well, the apostle makes it perfectly plain and clear that it has. The answer is, the gift of the Holy Spirit – what the Holy

Spirit does to us and in us, and what he enables us to do. This is the great thing that the apostle holds before us here and to which I am now directing your attention. The way in which the apostle puts this is extremely interesting. (We are concentrating at this point especially on verse 7.) 'God', he said, 'hath not given us the spirit of fear; but of power, and of love, and of a sound mind' (or of discipline). He put it like that because the trouble with Timothy at that time was that he was suffering from what one may call 'the spirit of fear'. So the Apostle said, 'You know, we were not meant to be like that, that is not the spirit that we have been given.' But that was Timothy's condition, and when a man is defeated by life it is always due, ultimately, to the fact that he is suffering from this spirit of fear.

Now, I want to try to show you that, in fact, this spirit of fear is the real, the ultimate cause of all failure in life, and of all unhappiness. This is the thing that gets us down, and that defeats us all by nature. Read Genesis 3 which seems to me to be such a perfect summary of the whole story of the human race. We are shown very clearly there that the first result of the fall of man was fear. God had made man in his own image. He had made him perfect, he had put him in Paradise, and there was nothing that man in that condition enjoyed more than the company of God. He was made for communion with God and he enjoyed it. So that when man heard the voice of God coming into the garden, he rushed to meet him, and there was nothing that gave him greater pleasure. But after that act of rebellion and disobedience and defiance of God you remember what happened – the moment they had sinned, they were filled with fear. They found they were naked, and they were filled with a spirit of fear. They went to hide themselves in the trees, and they heard the voice of the Lord God, calling out 'Adam, where art thou?' Adam and Eve emerged trembling, frightened, alarmed, and Adam said, in all honesty, 'I heard thy voice . . . and I was afraid'. For the first time in their lives Adam and Eve were filled with a spirit of fear. There had been no fear in Eden until this act of disobedience.

Now this is the whole philosophy of life. It is, in a sense, the essence of the whole of the biblical teaching. Man has always thought that he can obtain liberty and happiness, satisfaction and peace and joy by rebelling against God. That is the popular teaching today and it is a repetition of the first sin. People say, 'Do not be interested any longer in this religion, what is it? Ah, it is the dope of the masses, the opiate of the people, call it what you like.' While others say, 'Of course, religion and the Church have held people down in the past because they have used this weapon of fear. They have filled people with terror and alarm, and have held them before the wrath of an angry God; and so men and women in their ignorance were afraid and believed it, and were nothing more than slaves.'

And the people who say this fondly believe that the way to find emancipation and freedom and peace and rest, liberty and enjoyment, and the loss of all fear of life, is to turn your back upon God and to rebel and to live your own life in your own way. But, the whole biblical case is that it works exactly the other way round, that it is because man turns away from God that he gets possessed by the spirit of fear; that there never would have been fear at all in the human race were it not for man's fall and departure from God. That is what brought in this element of fear and it is with us still. Furthermore, I want to try to show you that it is the main and dominant element in the life of this world at this very moment, and it is the main cause why so many people are utterly defeated.

The apostle, then, puts it like this to Timothy. Timothy, he says, in effect, 'you know you are behaving exactly as if you were not a Christian. That is how I expect a man who is not a Christian to react to what is happening to me, and to what may happen to you. But,' he says, 'God hath not given us (who are Christians) the spirit of fear, that is the spirit of the world.' Now, the Apostle had to say this very often. He says exactly the same thing in slightly different language to the Romans when he writes to them like this: 'For ye have not received the spirit of bondage again to fear; but ye have received the Spirit of adoption, whereby we cry, Abba, Father', which is exactly the same thing.

We must examine this together, and so let me take as my first point the causes of this spirit of fear. This is the trouble in life, that men and women are afraid. What are we afraid of by nature? Of course, I am ready to grant that there is in many cases an individual or personal element. We are not all the same. Thank God we are not! There are some people who are more fearful by nature than others. As I have told you, this young man Timothy was obviously a case of that, and, I believe, the same was true of the apostle Paul himself by nature, as a natural man. That element does come in. We need not stay with that because the whole case of the gospel is to say that it does not matter what you are by nature.

Now, I hope I have made that perfectly clear. I tried to bring out that point when we began our consideration of this passage. Here, in this realm, it does not matter at all what our natural make-up is. There is nothing more wonderful to me about the long history of the Christian Church than the way in which we find in the same Church, sharing the same experience, men and women of every conceivable type of temperament, psychology, personality, call it what you like. You have your optimists and pessimists, you have your sanguine, hopeful people, and then you have other people who always look at the darker side, you have your mercurial people, your phlegmatic people. Oh, thank God for this! It does not matter what we are.

And let me add to that – it does not matter what a man's nationality is. Nationality does make a difference and it is important. Every man who belongs to any nationality has got things to fight in particular that others have not, and he may have strength that others have not, but it does not matter at all when he comes to the Christian church, whatever he is. Whatever the colour of his skin, whatever his background, whatever his cultural antecedents – it does not matter at all. We are dealing here with the power of God, with what God can do to a man, and what God can make of him. I am granting that the individual make-up plays a part. Everybody has got some peculiar something to fight above everything else. It is not always the same but we are all enabled to fight by the same means. That is the message.

Let us, therefore, look at the more general causes of this spirit of fear. I am asserting that this is one of the most fearful generations that the world has ever known, that there is nothing more obvious about the life of this country and of the world today than this spirit of fear. And, I would suggest that the first cause of this is what we may call finitude, man's consciousness of the fact that he is finite. Or, if you like, the fact that he is so small.

Now it is not surprising that this should be the cause, and a very prolific one, of much fear in this present age and generation. We are living in what is called an expanding universe. The psalmist, even in his day, was able to say, 'When I consider thy heavens, the work of thy fingers, the moon and the stars . . . what is man, that thou art mindful of him?' And he did not know much about science, did he? We now know so much more about science. We see this expanding universe, and hear the scientists talking about billions of light years and these tremendous distances, and these great powers and forces – and, of course, we cannot hear about these things or read about them without feeling that we are very small. This is the extraordinary contradiction in modern man; he is very big when he looks at himself intellectually and thinks he can encompass the whole cosmos; and then when he thinks of these powers in what Sir James Jeans called 'this mysterious universe' he feels so small. The vastness of space, those illimitable distances, the Milky Way, there in that vastness which is without end as it were – what, then, is man? Finitude! And, surely, a man who really thinks at all must be frightened by all this, for it is a very alarming thought.

Let me expand that a little. Take then all these unseen forces and powers that have been discovered, and in a sense released, by science; think of the tremendous power and the force in an atom. It is the splitting of the atom that has released atomic power, and when we think that the whole cosmos is made up of this tremendous power and force, living in that almost indescribable tension, we begin to feel afraid and we wonder where we stand, living in such a world. When we hear a thunderclap, does it not frighten us? There is something tremendously frightening about it – this unseen power, this electric force, these explosions! And here are we in a vast, tremendous world like this. Now this is a part of what I am describing as the finitude of man.

And then what brings it right home to us, of course, is our realisation of our ignorance. While we are boasting about our advance in knowledge, there is a sense in which it is equally true to say that the more our knowledge advances the more we are discovering how little we know. We do not understand it. The universe is mysterious. And we discover this bit and that bit and we get very excited, but oh, what we do not understand! It is like an iceberg. We have just discovered the little bit that is out above the surface but nine-tenths of it is down below, and who knows what that is? So we begin to say with Tennyson:

> Our little systems have their day,
> They have their day and cease to be;
> They are but broken lights of thee
> And thou, O God, art more than they.

How little we understand, how small are our little philosophies after all. Man is thus made to feel his finitude. It is exactly like a man being out in some unknown place in the dark, wondering what is there, what is behind that hedge, what may be coming round that corner, and not knowing. Or it is like a man in a little yacht or a small rowing boat, in a great ocean, battling with billows and unfathomable powers so infinitely greater than himself. That is how man feels by nature. The moment he begins to explore his universe he is impressed by nothing other than his sense of finitude.

The other factor in man's sense of fear is, I think, the meaninglessness and the purposelessness of life. I am talking now about a man who is not a Christian – because, you see, these very scientists who tell us about this great and mysterious universe may well be the same people who are telling us that life is meaningless and purposeless and that there is no object in it all, that it leads to nothing. They cannot prophesy anything; they cannot tell us with assurance that the world is going to get better and better. Some of them do, but the realists among them tell us that they cannot say that, because they are not entitled to do so. It is to them all being governed by some blind impersonal force and they do not know what such a force is going to do: it may strengthen, it may weaken. It may improve in yet more wonderful forms or it may explode everything, and that would be the end – they do not know. There is no mind, there is no person behind it all.

So, the modern man has been taught this and he feels that life is meaningless, without purpose. And then he says, 'Well, why should I live? What is the point of it? There is nothing to strive for, no objective to make for.' And all this leads to a kind of slackness and indolence, which in turn leads to a spirit of fear. Because as long as you ask, as it were, 'What is the use of anything?' and say 'There is no point in striving if it is all going to end in nothing', or perhaps 'I do not know what it is going to end in', then you sit down and do nothing. But these other forces and powers are still there, and your indolence and the vastness we saw earlier come together again and increase your sense of fear.

And then add to all this the sense of insecurity. There is nothing that is so frightening as a sense of insecurity; the fear of the unknown. Here you are; thanking God for all your knowledge. And then you begin to think, 'What if I am suddenly taken ill? I am enjoying life, everything is very wonderful. I am surrounded by wife and family, everything is going well in an affluent society. But what if I am taken ill? What if I lose my health, or suffer some grievous loss? Life is so insecure.' There is the unknown, you never know what is going to happen. Life is full of such tremendous possibilities. You cannot forecast, you do not know what is coming; people rush to fortune tellers because they want to know. They cannot tell them either, but that is why there is this interest in astrology today. It is the fear of the unknown trying to find out – 'How many years have I got left, what is the future going to be like? If only I knew I could do something, but I do not know.' And you cannot know. There is a fear of the unknown, of illness, of loss, or the possibility of another war – war which shatters plans and purposes.

Then, we are being told increasingly that there is a terrible possibility of world famine! Because of the population explosion, and because of the erosion of the soil, because the population by the year 2000 is going to be double what it was in the early 'fifties, there is not going to be enough food for everybody. We are faced with the possibility of famine. And there, always in the background, is the fact of death.

Now, all these things conspire together to fill man with a sense of fear, and yet I have not given the main and ultimate explanation of this spirit of fear. It is all there in Genesis 3. The real reason why man is fearful as the result of these factors is that he was made to be dependent upon God. He was placed in this vast, endless cosmos; yes, but he was not put alone in it. It was not like landing a child on a doorstep, or putting a man out in the mid-Atlantic and leaving him alone in his little, frail bark. No, no, man was not alone, he was made for God by God, and in communion with God, in fellowship with God. He was in this expanding, endless universe but in touch with the maker and creator. Man was made in such a way that he was to be dependent upon God. And the whole trouble with man in sin, the whole trouble with modern man, is that he is not big enough for the position into which he has put himself. Modern man is like many a man who has lived in this world, the kind who has got an inflated notion of his own powers and capacities, and who applies for a job that is too big for him. He is all right in his department, as a second-in-command, or lower down the line. As long as he has got somebody above him who understands the whole business, he is all right as an executive, as a man who can carry out; but the man has got an inflated notion about himself. Many a young man in a family business has done this and has lost his job. To the older men, whom his father put into the business, he says, 'I can do all this myself,' and he puts himself in the chairman's seat. But he is not big enough and the whole business goes wrong; 'He is too big for his boots,' as we say, because he has taken on a position that he cannot handle, he cannot manage, and he ends up floundering.

Now you have known this in life many times, have you not? People have this inflated notion of themselves, and this is what man has done. Man has said, 'I do not need God, I am capable of understanding and running the cosmos.' And modern man is trying to run the cosmos, but he cannot. Things keep on going wrong in this department and that. There is an explosion, or an accident, there is a death, there is a loss, and man is alarmed and frightened and the whole machinery is going wrong. He is not big enough, he does not look down upon it, he has not got the control – he was never meant to be in control. God is the controller of the universe, and no wonder man is frightened. He is like a man entering into some great machine house, confident that because he has read a book or two, he will be able to run the whole machinery: and there he sees levers: which does he pull and which does he not pull? Something is happening over there, but he cannot be here, there and everywhere! So he becomes alarmed and terrified waiting for the whole thing to blow up. That, according to the whole teaching of the Bible, is the picture of man in this world since the fall. That is the spirit of fear. Man has taken on the universe but he is not big enough to do so. He is too big for his boots, and the result is that he has now arrived at the point of crisis and he does not know what he is doing.

That, then, leads me to my second principle, which I put in this form. If those are the causes of fear, what are its consequences? And now we come, I think, to the very essence of the modern problem. This is a very, very relevant section of scripture. The first consequence of fear is always weakness. Fear is paralysing. Have you not often used the expression, 'paralysed by fear'? It does something to you, it knocks you on the head, as it were, it paralyses your brain, making you feel limp and weak, and ready to collapse, and many do actually collapse and faint. If you are afraid of an animal, the animal will soon know it. Have you ever been on the back of a horse that you have been afraid of? I can assure you the horse soon realises it, he knows your weakness. Fear always leads to weakness and lack of control. And the apostle tells Timothy that he is behaving in an utterly weak manner. Timothy is whimpering and crying, and sending letters to Paul, because he does not know what to do. Now that is because he is afraid. If you are afraid, I say again, of a task that is allotted to you, so long as you are governed by the spirit of fear, you will not be able to do that job. You have got to get rid of fear before you can do anything. Fear always paralyses.

Secondly, it always leads – and this is an extraordinary thing about fear – to selfishness. The fearful person is always a selfish person because, you see, he is afraid of what is going to happen to him, or she is afraid of what is going to happen to her. It leads to an idea of self-protection, self-preservation, and that in turn leads to antagonism to others. Fear puts you on edge. You become ill at ease, wondering what is going to happen to you. In that state you are touchy, and if somebody makes a noise, as always happens, they irritate you, so you find fault with them, and you are always in trouble. You are filled with this irritability which is always an outcome of selfishness. Fear invariably does this. You look at a child suffering from fear and it will become peevish and difficult to handle. The child cannot help it. And mistakes are often made even in medical diagnoses along this very line. There are people who come with this symptom or that, but their real trouble is that they are afraid of something. Fear can show itself in an almost endless variety of ways, physical, mental, moral, spiritual and everything else: and in weakness or selfishness. And then, of course, inevitably, in unhappiness and misery. You cannot be at one and the same time fearful and happy. So you see the very spirit of fear is a great cause of the unhappiness that is in the world today.

But the thing I want to emphasise above everything else at this point is that fear always leads to irrationality. Fear does really paralyse, and it paralyses the brain above everything else; and because it does so, the brain does not function properly and this leads to people acting in an utterly irrational manner. In other words, there is nothing that makes people behave with such irresponsibility as the spirit of fear. It has always done this. Watch people in a condition of fear – they will do the most amazing and extraordinary things and not know why they are doing them. Why? Because their fear has made them irrational.

And, of course, it leads in the same way to escapism. Now, I want to be very practical here, and to show you the relevance of what the apostle is saying to the conditions in this world at this very moment. How is the spirit of fear manifesting itself in this present generation? Well, its most obvious manifestation is the pleasure mania. Why is everybody plunging into pleasure? There is only one answer. It is a part of the escape mechanism – the fear of life.

I think I have quoted this before, but this is a sheer fact of history. At the beginning of the last war, when the black-out regulations were brought in, all theatres, all cinemas and places of amusement were shut, by order of the government. I have never forgotten what happened as a result, because it was such a proof of what the Bible says. There was a constant stream of protest in the newspapers, and in every other way conceivable, urging the authorities to open the cinemas again and the theatres and the places of amusement. And this was because people had discovered – and it was a very good bit of psychological observation – that if men and women were going to be kept at home every night without having the release of the cinema and the theatre and the other places of amusement, they would not be able to take the strain of war, they would not stand up to it. So the theatres and the cinemas were opened, if I remember rightly, after three or four nights of being shut, because of the public outcry and demand. Why did this happen? Escapism! It is a terrible thing to the modern man to be compelled to sit in his own house for a week at a time and just to think and face life, and the facts of life and its possibilities: he cannot do it. So he escapes via pleasure in its various forms.

And, of course, the same thing happens with drink. Even

when there is a war and when the ships are being sunk, and when the whole question of feeding this nation may arise, there is very little restriction on drink. Why? Well, the statesmen know perfectly well that this country cannot be kept going without drink, the morale of the country would collapse without it.

And then we have it today in the form of drugs – purple-hearts, so-called pep-pills, stimulants . . . What is the matter with people, why do they need them? It is all because they are afraid. Do not misunderstand me, I am not here to condemn men and women, I am sorry for them. I am a preacher of the gospel because I am sorry for people who cannot go on without drugs and drinks and pleasure and all these things. And of course we are seeing even more today; we are seeing outbreaks of hysteria, mass hysteria. I am sorry for the young people of today with this sense of finitude, with this sense of utter purposelessness, with these atomic and hydrogen bombs in the background. They are really terrified, they are afraid of life – so what do they do? Well, they must let go somehow and so they become hysterical, and you get the hysteria aroused by these poor pop stars and their followers, and others like them. Do not laugh at them, you ought to weep for them: you should weep for them! This hysteria is a disease, a spirit of fear, leading to utter irrationality; life has lost any meaning or purpose for such people, and this is how it is showing itself. It is an explosion of man in the grip of the spirit of fear. He has no answer, no solution at all.

There, according to the biblical teaching, is what all this spirit of fear leads to. And ultimately it leads in many cases to despair, often to suicide, because people cannot stand up to it any longer. They just say, 'I cannot! I must go out!' – and out they go. It is all the result of the spirit of fear. Man in the grip of the spirit of fear becomes irrational, and so, irresponsible. When a man is in the grip of a spirit of fear, be ready for him to do anything that is conceivable. He will do any kind of madness, because he does not know what he is doing.

And I believe that this generation to which you and I belong, and these immediate present days in particular, are giving us the most perfect demonstration of the truth of the biblical teaching that perhaps the world has ever known. We are seeing the spirit of fear in this manifestation of utter irrationality. I am not here to blame these poor people, I am here to tell them that there is only one cure for it all, only one answer. What is it? What have I got to say to a world in fear, a world that is terrorised and irrational and behaving as it is? I am here to say this – there is only one answer.

What, then, is it? It is not 'pull yourself together'. There is nothing more idiotic to say to a poor person who is in the grip of the spirit of fear than 'pull yourself together'. That is the one thing he cannot do. If he could he would. And yet, that is what the world says, not the clever world but the stupid world, which believes in a sort of muscular outlook upon life: 'Pull yourself together'! You cannot say that to a person who is suffering from melancholia, or hysteria, or any of these things. They cannot do it, they are beyond that, they are in the grip of fear, they are irrational. And it is no use addressing an appeal to the rational element of a person who is irrational. That, incidentally, for the sake of you philosophers, is the whole weakness in the entire position of Bertrand Russell. He says man is irrational, and then he appeals to his rationality. And that is why he is finally such a profound pessimist about the whole future of the human race. You cannot have it both ways, yet that is what he tries to do.

Neither is the answer to be found in the teaching of the cults – the power of positive thinking, for example. Now, do not misunderstand me. I am not here to say that the cults, and psychology, and all these things do not help people up to a point, but they do not really help fundamentally; they only drug us for the time being. Christian Science tells us that there is no such thing as matter, and because that is so, there cannot be such a thing as a disease; and, therefore, when we think we are ill, we are not, and what we have got to do is to tell ourselves that we are not ill because we cannot be. But we know that Mrs Mary Baker Eddy, at the end of her life, had to take morphia and to use spectacles. It is all right in theory, and of course it will cover a lot of aches and pains. Christian

Science, and all the cults, are quite good in dealing with many functional diseases, as they are called, that is with ailments which are not organic; but when they come to the organic, of course, they do nothing, and the patient dies. Mrs Baker Eddy herself sent for a doctor, a blank contradiction of all her teaching! Ah yes, these things may be all right up to a point, but they do not deal with the fundamental questions with which we are dealing. The answer to the problem is not, then, some cult, or psychology, or Couéism, or some general optimistic idealistic philosophy. The two world wars have really knocked the bottom out of all those, and it is because they have done so that we are getting this terrible hysterical reaction, I think, out of this present generation.

'God,' says Paul, 'has not given us any of those things. He has given us the Holy Spirit, and he is not a spirit of fear, but a spirit "of power, and of love, and of a sound mind".' You notice the apostle keeps on saying this. He says, 'Stir up the gift of God, which is in thee by the putting on of my hands . . . That good thing which was committed unto thee keep by the Holy Ghost which dwelleth in us.' Here is Christianity! It is not only forgiveness, it is not only rebirth, it goes beyond all that; it tells us that God puts the Holy Spirit into us; that the Spirit 'dwells' in us. 'If any man have not the Spirit of Christ, he is none of his.' The Christian is enabled in all respects by the Spirit that dwells in him. I think this is the most wonderful thing of all. We are not left to ourselves; to use again my earlier illustration, what this gospel does is to bring us back, if you like, into the relationship which we once had with the general manager. We are no longer heads of the universe, but we are back in our rightful positions and he is in control. He tells us what to do, he gives us authority, he gives us power, and he does it all through giving us his Spirit.

In other words, this is the glory of this message, that a man is not left to himself, but is given the Spirit of the living God. 'God hath not given us the spirit of fear; but of power, and of love, and of a sound mind.' But notice this. The Holy Spirit is not some power that operates in us automatically. There are people who believe that, and they turn Christianity into a cult.

You get it in a meeting, they say, and that means that you have always got it. But that is not true. Timothy has to be told this: 'I put thee in remembrance that thou stir up the gift . . .' There is man's side in this. It is not passive, it is not something done for us. Man has got to 'stir up the gift' that is in him. He is given the gift of the Spirit, but he must realise that and obey the leading of the Spirit, and go on in the strength and the power of the Spirit.

And as he does so what will happen to him? He will be given the very antidote to everything that results from fear. 'God hath not given us the spirit of fear', but of 'power'. Power! God's power! God's power working in us and enabling us! 'Work out your own salvation with fear and trembling.' Why? 'For it is God which worketh in you both to will and to do of his good pleasure.' We are not left alone to battle with the world and the flesh and the devil. We could not do it. But God's Spirit comes within us and he is a Spirit of power. He can keep us, he can enable us, he works in us, he transforms us and everything that is round and about us. This is the great hope of the Christian, that he is not left to himself.

Now, the apostle works this out in a most wonderful manner in Romans 8: 'What shall we then say to these things?' he asks. And here is his answer: 'If God be for us, who can be against us?' 'If God be for us' – and he is for us if we believe in Christ, and he puts his Spirit into us – 'If God be for us, who can be against us? He that spared not his own son, but delivered him up for us all, how shall he not with him also freely give us all things? Who shall lay anything to the charge of God's elect? It is God that justifieth. Who is he that condemneth? It is Christ that died, yea rather, that is risen again, who is even at the right hand of God, who also maketh intercession for us.' Then hear this: 'Who shall separate us from the love of Christ?' There is the challenge. 'Shall tribulation, or distress, or persecution, or famine, or nakedness, or peril, or sword? As it is written, For thy sake we are killed all the day long; we are accounted as sheep for the slaughter. Nay, in all these things we are more than conquerors through him that loved us. For I am persuaded, that neither death, nor life, nor angels, nor principalities, nor powers, nor things present, nor things to come, nor height, nor depth, nor any other creature, shall be able to separate us from the love of God, which is in Christ Jesus our Lord.' Neither life, nor Nero, nor prison, nor death, nor anything – nothing! Why? Because it is the power of God. As the hymn says:

> His power subdues our sin,
> And his forgiving love
> Far as the east is from the west
> Doth all our sins remove.

Or take another –

> He breaks the power of cancelled sin
> He sets the prisoner free.

'If the Son shall make you free', says our Lord himself, 'you shall be free indeed.'

> I need thee every hour, stay thou near by;

Why? Because –

> Temptations lose their power when thou art nigh.

> Guide me, O thou great Jehovah,
> Pilgrim through this barren land;
> I am weak, but thou art mighty,
> Hold me with thy powerful hand:
> Bread of heaven,
> Feed me now and evermore.

> When I tread the verge of Jordan
> Bid my anxious fears subside;
> Death of death, and hell's destruction,
> Land me safe on Canaan's side:
> Songs of praises
> I will ever give to thee.

Or take George Matheson's great hymn. What a perfect statement it is of all this.

Make me a captive, Lord,
And then I shall be free;

'I have tried to be the general manager of the universe, and I am alarmed, I am frightened, I am terrified. Put me back in the office', says the office boy. 'As long as I know that you are in the main office all is well.'

Make me a captive, Lord,
And then I shall be free;

I can then do what I was meant to do, as long as I know that you are at the controls.

Force me to render up my sword,
And I shall conqueror be.

I sink in life's alarms
While by myself I stand;
Imprison me within thine arms,
And strong shall be my hand.

My heart is weak and poor
Until its master find;
It has no spring of action sure,
It varies with the wind.

It cannot freely move
Till thou hast wrought its chain;
Enslave it with thy matchless love,
And deathless it shall reign.

My will is not my own
Till thou hast made it thine;
If it would reach a monarch's throne . . .

And that is where we all want to be, is it not? But we cannot put ourselves there. The whole of civilisation has been trying to put itself on a monarch's throne, and it realises it is a buffoon.

> If it would reach a monarch's throne
> It must its crown resign.

It must throw its own self-made tawdry crown to the scrap-heap of eternity, and receive the crown of righteousness that the Lord alone can give.

> It only stands unbent
> Amid the clashing strife,
> When on thy bosom it has leant,
> And found in thee its life.

You are offered here a spirit of power, the power of God taking hold of you, surrounding you, enabling you, ever with you. I care not, therefore, what man may say or do to me, because God has said, 'I will never leave thee, nor forsake thee.' 'Imprison me within thine arms, And strong shall be my hand.' 'Make me a captive, Lord, And then I shall be free.' 'The spirit of power, and of love'! Oh, how it answers all the things that are produced by the spirit of fear!

I have already shown that fear always makes us selfish, it also makes us irritable and difficult to live with. A frightened person is an object of compassion; he feels that everything, the whole world and the universe, is against him. And he hates it in turn, and so he is unhappy and makes others unhappy. But, you see, we are told here that we are given a spirit of 'love', and you know what that is. You remember how our Lord put it in the Sermon on the Mount: 'Ye have heard that it was said by them of old time,' Do good to them that love you; be kind to those who are kind to you; love those who love you, 'Thou shalt love thy neighbour, and hate thine enemy.' Then he goes on 'But I say unto you, Love your enemies, bless them that curse you, do good to them that hate you, and pray for them which despitefully use you, and persecute you; That ye may be the children of your father which is in heaven: for he maketh his sun to rise on the evil and on the good, and sendeth rain on the just and on the unjust. For if ye love them which love you, what reward have ye? do not even the publicans the same? And if ye salute your brethren only, what do ye more than others? do not even the publicans so? Be ye therefore perfect, even as your father which is in heaven is perfect.'

This is indeed a spirit of love, enabling a man to love his enemies, delivering him from fear and all the irritability and the enmity created by fear. It makes him feel sorry even for his enemies and those who malign him and persecute him. You remember what our blessed Lord said when they nailed him to the cross? He said, 'Father, forgive them; for they know not what they do.' He was not frightened, and because he was not frightened he did not hate the people who were responsible for his crucifixion. He was the son of God, he knew he was in the hands of the eternal and he could say, 'Father, forgive these people, who have done this to me, for they know not what they do.' That is the spirit of love.

Is it possible in a man? Yes, but only when he is filled with the Holy Spirit. There is a glorious example of this in Acts, in a man called Stephen. We are told of Stephen in the seventh chapter, that he was 'full of the Holy Ghost', and this is how he showed it: cruel men stoned him to death for nothing. The Pharisees and Sadducees and religious authorities, literally stoned him to death, and these were the words upon his dying lips: 'Lord, lay not this sin to their charge.' Why? Well, he was not afraid. Stephen was the only man on that occasion who was not afraid. These other people had felt something of the power of the gospel. They had seen his face shining as he was addressing the Sanhedrin conference. They felt the power of the spirit and they were terrified, and men in that position always act irrationally. They murdered him! They were terrified, but the man who was being stoned to death was perfectly at peace. He was sorry for them, he prayed for them and he said. 'Lord, lay not this sin to their charge.' He had got the spirit of love as well as the spirit of power.

And, lastly, the Holy Spirit gives us a 'sound mind' – discipline. Oh, this is wonderful. Self-control! When the Holy Spirit is in us and operating in us, whatever may happen to us, we do not react violently, we do not lose our heads and panic and lose control and say, 'What is happening? If God is a God of love why has this happened to me?' We do not feel that the end of the world has come, and rush about frantically and do irrational things. No, no! The man who has the Spirit of God operating in him is not only made strong, he is not only made loving, he is made rational. The only man who really can understand the history of the world is a Christian. You see the modern world does not understand. We read in our papers, for example, that a committee is to be set up to enquire into a new outbreak of violence. Why? Well, because they do not understand. They do not understand why people are behaving like this; and it is only the Holy Spirit who can give us the explanation. Man apart from God will always act like that in some shape or form; he has always been doing it. The manifestations vary, but the thing in principle is always the same. And it is the Spirit who gives us discipline, a sound mind and self-control, so that we understand what is happening.

I put it like this to you. What the apostle is really saying to Timothy, in effect, is this: 'Timothy, did you ever really imagine that the whole world would be delighted to hear my preaching? Are you really surprised that they have put me into prison and that they are threatening to put me to death? Are you surprised at that? Timothy, where is your understanding? You are reacting to events. Why do you not look down upon them; why do you not have the mind of Christ in operation; why do you not see that man in sin is in a sense bound to act like this; the gospel is foolishness to him, and in his blindness, he sees it as something against him. He thinks God is against him. He thought the son of God was against him. He is only behaving irrationally. Look down upon it,

Timothy, and you will not be surprised, you will see through it all. Let the Spirit lead you to understand it.'

The Spirit of God not only enables us to understand all these things and to see through them, it enables us, thank God, to see beyond them. And that, God willing, is the thing I am hoping to direct your attention to next. 'I am not ashamed.' Why not? Because 'I know whom I have believed, and am persuaded that he is able to keep that which I have committed unto him against that day' – and a man who has had a glimpse of that day is never again afraid of anything that can happen to him in this present, passing, evil world.

My dear friends, is the Spirit of God in you? What is the spirit that is dominating your life at this moment? This is a very practical thing. I am not speaking theoretically, thank God. What is the dominating spirit in you? Are you afraid? Are you terrified by your finitude, by the uncertainty, by the seen, by the unseen, the knowable and the unknowable? Or have you got the spirit of power and of love, and of a sound mind? If you have not got it, all you need to do is to come to God without delay just as you are. Admit and confess your folly and your failure, believe his message concerning his son Jesus Christ, the Saviour, who has been manifested, who has abolished death and brought life and immortality to light through his gospel. Believe on him as the son of God who died for your sins, to reconcile you to God and to make you a child of God and an heir of heaven; commit yourself to him and he will put his spirit into you. His spirit is a spirit of power, and of love, and of a sound mind, and he will deliver you from the spirit of fear and all the irrationality that always results from fear.

Beloved people, do not give yourselves rest or peace until you get to know him, this blessed son of God. He has gone through it all, he has conquered everything, he has opened the way even into the glory of eternity. Get to know him, so that, whatever happens to you, you will be able to say, 'Nevertheless I am not ashamed: for I know whom I have believed, and am persuaded that he is able to keep that which I have committed unto him against that day.'

Chapter Ten

SUNDAY EVENING SERMON
14th June 1964

'That Day'

For the which cause I also suffer these things: nevertheless I am not ashamed: for I know whom I have believed, and am persuaded that he is able to keep that which I have committed unto him against that day (2 Tim. 1:12).

The glory of the Christian message, as we have seen, is that a man is not left to himself but is given the Spirit of the living God. And, as I have been emphasising, the only way to conquer in this world, the only way to be master of life, is to believe this message. There is no patent remedy here; I have got nothing that I can give you. I suppose, if I were so disposed, I could do certain things to you. It is not difficult, you know, to play psychologically with people. I could, but I do not want to. If I just made you feel happy for the moment, well, I would be a hindrance to the gospel, and God forgive me if ever I am guilty of that. I am not to do anything to you of myself; all I am to do is to lead you to the gospel, to lead you to the glory of the Lord of the gospel, to remind you of the truth concerning him. So, you see, I do not want to do anything in order to produce a kind of psychological effect. No, it is the truth alone. The truth that our Lord would preach sitting in a boat or sitting on the side of a mountain. You do not need any adventitious aids with this gospel, it is the truth itself. And the business of preaching is just to present the truth to men and women. Paul says to Timothy, in effect, 'I am what I am, and I am not ashamed though I am in these circumstances, because I believe what I believe; and you must do the same.'

And in the whole of the passage from verses six to fourteen, the apostle takes the trouble to divide up this great truth, to give a summary of Christian doctrine, so that the dejected Timothy may come back to it and be clear about it. There is only one gospel. This is an exclusive gospel. We do not need a world congress of faiths. The Christian faith needs no help, it needs no addition. Not any of the other religions, so-called, have got anything to give us; we do not need them. Here is the one and only gospel, and so the apostle tells Timothy to hold it fast, and that if he does so all will be well with him. And you and I, my friends, have got to learn to do the same thing.

So we must know this everlasting gospel, and what I want to emphasise again is this, that we must know it as a whole, we must know it all. We cannot take parts out of the gospel and get the real blessing; we must take it all, we must take it as it is. The glory of this gospel is that it is a complete whole. That is what amazes me and astounds me more and more the more I read it and study it as year passes year – I am more amazed at this gospel tonight than I have ever been, I am more thrilled by it for the same reason. What a complete philosophy it is! Nothing can ever happen that is not catered for. It is a round, a whole, a massive, a gigantic view of all things, and we must take it all.

And so we have been looking at parts of it and we come now to what seems to me to be the ultimate doctrine. We have been looking at the doctrine of man, Paul's emphasis upon the soul, our relationship to God, the person of the Lord Jesus Christ, this one who has been 'manifested', this one who has 'abolished death, brought life and immortality to light' – including all the doctrine of his death, his resurrection, the atonement. It is all here, it is a perfect summary. And then we hear of Christ as the redeemer, the nature of salvation. You notice even in a summary like this he has got to bring in again, 'not according to our works but according to his own purpose and grace'. That is how we are saved; that is the nature of the salvation. And then he goes on to tell us how it leads to forgiveness, it leads to new birth. We have been 'called with an holy calling', we are in a new life, and the Spirit is given to us and put into us, and we are delivered from the spirit of fear.

That, then, brings us to this last great element in the Christian doctrine, in the Christian teaching, and it is here in two words: 'that day'. 'I know whom I have believed, and am persuaded that he is able to keep that which I have committed unto him against *that day*.' I have said that it is important that we should believe the whole of Christian doctrine, and there is nothing more important, it seems to me, in this twentieth century than that we should know the Christian teaching about 'that day'.

Obviously it is one of the most vital things in the apostle's experience and is, perhaps, the note of all notes that is always being struck and held before us in New Testament teaching. You will notice that in this second epistle to Timothy, in chapter four, the apostle comes back to it again and he puts the same thing in a different way. 'I am now ready to be offered, and the time of my departure is at hand. I have fought a good fight, I have finished my course, I have kept the faith: henceforth there is laid up for me a crown of righteousness, which the Lord, the righteous judge, shall give me at that day: and not to me only, but unto all them also that love his appearing.' That day!

Then the book of Revelation, the last book in the Bible, is a book which really does nothing but give us an exposition of 'that day'. The whole of the Bible is pointing to a great day, and the thing which explains the kind of life that was lived by the New Testament Christians, and supremely by a man like this apostle, is their view of 'that day'. That was the thing that kept them going, that gave them their boldness and their courage, and that was the thing that made them ready to die. It was not an easy thing to be a Christian in the first century. In the Roman Empire they had to say that 'Caesar is Lord', and a Christian could not say that because he knew it was not true. The Christian knew that 'Jesus is Lord' and that there was no other Lord apart from Jesus. But he was told that if he did not

say that 'Caesar is Lord' he would be put to death, he would
be thrown to the lions in the arena.

What did these early Christians do? They did not hesitate
for a second; they said 'Jesus is Lord'! What enabled them to
say it? It was their view of 'that day'. It is the thing that makes
the apostle say here, in prison, 'I do not care what this man
does to me, this man Nero, this particular present Caesar; I
am thinking of that day, my eye is there.' It is the thing that
enables him to say, 'nevertheless I am not ashamed'. We
simply cannot understand the New Testament unless we
understand this doctrine about 'that day'. It was what sustained these people and made them the marvellous people
that they were. This was the thing that ultimately shook the
Roman Empire and the ancient world. There was something
about these Christians that enabled them to live and to die in a
way that Greek philosophy had never enabled anyone to do.
Many of the philosophers committed suicide, in spite of all
their great brains and thinking. But here were people who
seemed to be masters of life and of death. This was the thing
that really shook the ancient world; it was, to a great degree,
this faith of the Christians in this last day – this 'day'.

Indeed I can go further and I can say that the essential
message of even the Old Testament is exactly the same. Read
the Old Testament, go through the history of the children of
Israel, and read particularly the story of some of their most
outstanding men and characters. What was it that explained
them? Well, if you consult the author of the epistle to the
Hebrews, he gives a great portrait gallery of them in the
eleventh chapter; people like Abel, and Noah, and Enoch,
people like Abraham and Moses, these giants of men. What
was their secret? The author lets us into the secret and he puts
it like this. He says about Abraham, for instance, 'By faith he
sojourned in the land of promise, as in a strange country,
dwelling in tabernacles with Isaac and Jacob, the heirs with
him of the same promise'. Why did he do this? Because 'he
looked for a city which hath foundations, whose builder and
maker is God'. He then goes on and puts it still more plainly:
'These all died in faith, not having received the promises, but

having seen them afar off, and were persuaded of them, and embraced them, and confessed that they were strangers and pilgrims on the earth.'

Or take the case of a man like Moses. Here was a brilliant young man brought up as the son of Pharaoh's daughter, who had great prospects ahead of him. He put them all aside. Why? Because he belonged to these other people, these Jews, these Israelites, and so he had to endure all that we are told about, but he went through with it all – what is the secret? Listen! 'By faith Moses, when he was come to years, refused to be called the son of Pharaoh's daughter; choosing rather to suffer affliction with the people of God, than to enjoy the pleasures of sin for a season; esteeming the reproach of Christ greater riches than the treasures in Egypt: for he had respect unto the recompence of the reward. By faith he forsook Egypt, not fearing the wrath of the king: for he endured, as seeing him who is invisible.' That is the secret. It was the secret of all those giants of the faith even under the Old Testament, as well as the saints of the New Testament.

So, they all live, then, with their eye on 'that day'. That changes everything. They have a different perspective with regard to life. They do not live from hand to mouth or from day to day, they are not victims of history, man's history. They have another history and their eye is kept steadfastly on 'that day'. It is the great note of the whole of the Bible.

But not only that; it is the great note in all the most notable periods and epochs in the history of the Christian Church. What a story it is! Have you ever read the story of the martyrs and the confessors? I have mentioned some of them, those early Christians thrown to the lions in the arena in Rome and in other places. But persecution did not stop then; it went on, and we find the stories of martyrs throughout the running centuries. Have you heard the story of the Reformers? Have you ever read of the men who were burnt at the stake at Smithfield, and the martyrs who were burnt in Oxford? What accounts for these men? Why did they not give in to the religious and political authorities? Why did they stand against Mary – 'Bloody Mary' as she is so rightly called? Why did they not give in and save their lives? What is the secret? There is only one answer – they had their eye on 'that day', and 'the recompence of the reward'.

Come on to the Covenanters of the seventeenth century, the early Methodists and others, all ordinary people. The same is true of them. And, of course, that is why you get so much about this in the hymn books. The true New Testament Christian in every age and generation is a man who regards himself as a pilgrim and a stranger in this world. He says with Paul, 'our citizenship is in heaven', so he lives with 'that day' before him. It is the secret of the Church and its great people throughout the centuries.

But, as we all know, this is a doctrine that has been almost entirely neglected in this present century. We never hear of it. We are all consumed with a this-worldly outlook. Of course we have made fun of the other, have we not? The clever thing to do in this century, especially in the first half has been to scoff at 'pie-in-the-sky'. Why is this? Well, people said that what they wanted was to put this world right – it was the days of what they called 'the social gospel'. They really believed that the great Liberal administration of 1906 and onwards was going to usher in, to legislate in, the kingdom of God, the kingdom of heaven: knowledge and education and learning and science. They were going to banish war, they were all going to be friends, travel was made easier and they only needed to know one another to love one another. In this new century they were going to be emancipated, and so they stopped talking about 'that day' and they derided 'pie-in-the-sky'. They were going to make this a perfect world, and people really believed it. But it was completely shattered on August 4th, 1914, and the four terrible years that followed.

But this doctrine has still been lying in the background. Man still believes somehow that in spite of failure he can make this into a perfect world and that what we need is concentration on this world, to put it right and make it a better place.

Do not misunderstand me. Of course, we all believe in

making this a better world, and all of us who have any sense must believe in the rightness of political and social action. But – and it is this 'but' which is so important – that is not the main emphasis of the biblical teaching. Whether you and I like it or not, the Bible makes it abundantly plain and clear that this old world is an evil world and it is a damned one, it is a doomed world. This is Christian realism. According to the teaching of the Bible the most deluded person in the world today is the man who really believes that we can put this world right by political or social action. He is the biggest fool of all. It simply cannot be done, because human nature in sin is what it is. The whole story of civilisation is the story of man's attempt to make this world perfect. But he has never succeeded and he has never failed more than in this present century, when he seemed really to be on the very doorstep of final success.

But modern man still does not like this idea. He wants to live in this world and he wants it to be right. Now, there is only one answer to that: the hope is the world that is to come. 'That day.' And this is the big message. It is, surely, obvious, is it not? It is good when things are improved in this world, but we can pass all our Acts of Parliament and have the most perfect legislation imaginable, and still when we are taken ill as an individual or when we are disappointed in love, it will not help us very much. Though we have got a welfare state it does not comfort us, does it? When somebody who is dearer to us than life itself is taken away by death, we may have the most perfect surroundings but it does not help us.

In the great elemental problems, in the things that really matter, all the improvements man can introduce seem to be irrelevant, and of no use: and particularly in relation to the great fact of death itself. These things do not help us. Though we may have legislated for as perfect a world as is conceivable, when we have to make that final journey it does not help us. As I have sometimes said – a modern man makes preparation and arrangements for practically everything except his dying; he even makes arrangements for his funeral, but not for his dying. He takes an insurance to look after his burial, he will insure everything, make arrangements for everything except the most important thing of all, the very act of dying, and he never faces that; and that is the whole cause of the modern tragedy and the modern failure.

The answer, then, to it all is this doctrine of 'that day'. Let me try and summarise it for you. What does the apostle say: 'I . . . am persuaded that he is able to keep that which I have committed unto him against that day'. Does it just mean life after death? Does it just mean a future existence? Does it just mean the immortality of the soul? The answer of every one of the questions is no. They are all included but it means infinitely more. That is not the specific Christian doctrine about 'that day'.

The apostle, here in this verse, is referring to the teaching about the consummation of God's great plan and purpose for this world. Notice how he puts it. It is, of course, one of his leading themes everywhere. 'Who hath saved us, and called us with an holy calling, not according to his own purpose and grace, which was given us in Christ Jesus before the world began.' Now, that is the secret. The message of the Bible from beginning to end is just this: the unfolding of God's plan and purpose for this world. And that is why I rejoice to preach this gospel and stand in the pulpit as a great optimist in spite of all that is happening in the world, because I know that it is not left to us, to man. God is involved and God has a plan and a purpose. He is putting it into practice and he is going to end it. That is, 'that day', the end of history.

The trouble with all of us, Christian people included, is that we miss the wood because of the trees. As we read the Bible we get lost and immersed in details. We must always be careful about this; certainly, we must know the details. We must read the whole of the Bible, and we should read it at least once a year. But then, we must not stop at having just gone through the Bible. We must constantly stand back and say – what is it saying as a whole? And it is because people miss the whole that they get into trouble.

That is where Timothy was falling down. I have no doubt at all but that Timothy was all right about the doctrine of the

person of our Lord and about the way of redemption and
salvation. But he had forgotten 'that day'; he had forgotten
the purpose of God. I find so many like that today. There are
even evangelical people who put so much stress upon the
personal assurance of forgiveness and the fact that we may be
happy because our sins are forgiven, that they leave out the
world view of the gospel, this 'last day'; they leave out some of
the greatest glories. It is so selfish, so small, so personal. Of
course, the truth is personal, but it is not only personal, and if
you are living on the one experience you have had, or on your
feelings, you are going to be in trouble before long, when
things go wrong with you and when you have some trials and
tribulations, or when the devil is, as it were, let loose and
makes an onslaught upon you, you are going to be shaken to
your very foundations and you will wonder whether you are
Christians at all. The answer, the antidote, to all that, is to get
a whole view of the faith.

And nothing is more important in this connection
than that we should always hold the whole historical aspect
prominently in our minds. As I have said, I do not want you
just to look at the trees. I want you to see the wood, and I
know of nothing more exhilarating than to stand back and
look at it. What is the history? Let me give it to you in summary form: 'In the beginning God created'. There is the
start, the universe brought into being, set upon its course.
God starts history, he starts the time process. Creation!
Beginning!

Then, the next great event in history is the fall. There is that
perfect beginning and man is in Paradise and all is well and
man is happy. But we do not find him happy now, we cannot
say that all is well. Why not? Because of the fall – an event in
history – the fall of man. The Bible emphasises this. The
Lord Jesus Christ taught it. It is essential to an understanding
of the teaching of the apostle Paul's theology. I would not be
able to preach the gospel if I did not believe in the fall. I would
not understand why the world is as it is, were it not for the fall.
Moreover, I would not be able to stand up against all this
with any hope, if I did not know that though there was a fall,

God has a plan and a purpose to deal with the fall and its consequences.

And that is the great message of the Bible. The background is painted in the book of Genesis in just two chapters. The reason is that the Bible is essentially concerned about the history of salvation, and of redemption. So, we come to the fall in chapter three, which is followed by God coming in and giving the promise that the seed of the woman should bruise the serpent's head. Then the rest of the Old Testament is just increasing revelation about the outworking of this plan of God. He is going to send Someone, there is a deliverer coming: 'Comfort ye, comfort ye my people, saith your God.' Make a way for him in the wilderness. 'Every valley shall be exalted, and every mountain and hill shall be made low.' Make a highway for our Lord. This messiah is promised, and so everybody is looking forward to his coming.

Then we come to the great turning point in the whole of history. We come to what the New Testament calls 'the fulness of the times', to that which has changed BC into AD – this focal turning point in human history which has changed everything in the world. This is what the apostle is talking about here – '. . . but is now made manifest by the appearing of our Saviour Jesus Christ'. The birth of the babe of Bethlehem. That is one of the most staggering events of all history: 55 BC, 1066 – how trivial they are! They have made their little changes, but here is the thing that changes everything – time, eternity . . . The fulness of the times has come, God sends forth his son, made of a woman, made under the law, to redeem them that are under the law – that crucial period when the son of God was here in this world. 'The word' was made flesh! He lived, he died, was buried and rose again! This is shattering! The whole of history is affected by this.

Then we come to the present time, to everything that has happened since the son of God was in this world nineteen hundred years ago. According to the Bible, this is nothing but the outworking of what he came to do. God has this plan, this purpose, to save the world and to redeem a people unto himself, and the son of God came into the world in order to do what was essential before that could be done. God has got to punish sin, and yet how can he punish sin and save a man? There is only one way – he has got to punish somebody else who is big enough to take the punishment and not be destroyed by it; so the son of God was smitten in our stead, he died our death and our sins were laid upon him. That is why he died. That act on Calvary was the act of God making a way of salvation, 'that he might be just, and the justifier of him which believeth in Jesus' (Rom. 3:26).

The son, then, has made it possible, and he has gone back to heaven, and has sent the Spirit. And all that has been happening ever since is that God is calling out his people unto himself. In every age and generation there are men and women who believe this message and are born again. They become Christians and are added to the kingdom of God, and this number is being made up and up until the 'fulness' shall have arrived of Jew and Gentile: all saved in exactly the same way, the only way, by Jesus Christ and him crucified. There never has been a way of salvation apart from that, and there never will be. There is no future period to be when a Jew is going to save himself by believing. It is impossible! There is only one way, God's way and that is what is happening now.

But it is not the end; it is all leading up to a great consummation, what the apostle calls here, 'that day'. The process is going on. Paul says, in effect, 'I may go, others will come; they will go, others will come.' It will go on and on and on until 'that day' – and that is, the end. Now that end is as definite as was the beginning; as definite as was the fall; that end is as definite as was the birth of the babe of Bethlehem, his death, his resurrection, his ascension. 'That day'! It is a historical fact, it is actual, it will happen.

Now this is the biblical message. It gives us a complete review of history and brings us to the end. After that we have got nothing but eternity and its everlasting glory. Time has ended! 'Time shall be no more', and we will be in the eternal age.

'But what does this mean?' says somebody. 'What, then, is this "day", this "end" of which you are speaking?' I can only give you a summary of it, and perhaps this is the best thing to do. It is when people begin to dabble in details that they go so sadly astray, and some of them get so involved in details that they lose the main point. Some people are so expert about the details of the second coming, that they really do not give the glory to the Lord. They become immersed in some little detail that to them is of interest, and they are more interested in contemporary history than they are in the great consummation. Here is the summary; you will find it at the beginning of Acts 1: 'And when he had spoken these things, while they beheld, he was taken up; and a cloud received him out of their sight. And while they looked stedfastly toward heaven as he went up, behold, two men stood by them in white apparel; which also said, Ye men of Galilee, why stand ye gazing up into heaven? this same Jesus, which is taken up from you into heaven, shall so come in like manner as ye have seen him go into heaven. Then returned they unto Jerusalem from the mount called Olivet.' There is a summary of what is going to happen at the end.

'That day' means the day when the Lord Jesus Christ the son of God shall return again into this world. And this is something which is taught in the whole of the New Testament. It is all looking forward to it; the book of Revelation ends with it: 'Even so, come, Lord Jesus.' That is the cry.

It is sometimes called the 'appearing' or the 'epiphany' of our Lord. Take those first two chapters in the second epistle to the Thessalonians; there the apostle gives it an extended statement. Let me summarise it like this; this is what I can tell you about it from the scripture. That the Lord Jesus Christ will come again into this world in bodily form. 'He will so come even as you have seen him going,' said the two angels to the awestruck apostles as they stood there on mount Olivet. They were looking up into the heavens, they were amazed at the ascension. 'It is all right,' the two angels said, 'he will come back even as you have seen him go.' He will come in bodily form, he will come in visible form; 'every eye shall see him'. He will not come this time as the babe of Bethlehem. He will come as 'King of kings, and Lord of lords'. He will be 'riding the clouds of heaven'. He will be surrounded by a galaxy of holy angels. He will come in glory indescribable, with all the panoply of heaven and of glory manifesting his appearing.

Now the whole of the New Testament teaching is pointing to that, and when the apostle says, I am as I am because I know that he is 'able to keep that which I have committed unto him against that day' – the day of his coming, the day of his appearing, the day of his second coming out of the glory into this world of time – that is essentially what it means.

But let me go on. Why will he come? Why is it essential that we should believe this aspect of the message? And what is its further connotation? Well, the answer that is given is this: he will come again in that way because he must finish the work of redemption. 'But,' you say, 'did he not finish it on the cross?' In a sense he did. He finished the possibility of it on the cross, but it is not all finished. There God did the mightiest thing of all, there he reconciled the world unto himself through Jesus Christ; but there is still work to be done. Ever since then, the work of redemption has been continued, it has been applied, but it cannot be really finished without his coming back again. Why? Well, for this reason – and I know nothing more comforting and nothing more exhilarating than this – this world is God's world after all, it is not ours. And that is the tragedy of modern man, he seems to think that this is his world. It is not. He does not even understand it, it is all mysterious to him. It is God's world, it is God who made it and it belongs to God. And as I have reminded you, God made a perfect world, and do you ask me to believe that he is going to be content with allowing this world to go on like this? Can you imagine that the almighty glorious God is going to allow a world like this to go on for ever and for ever? Do you know what that would mean? It would mean that he had been defeated by the devil. God did not make the world as you and I see it. The world that you and I see is the world that has resulted from the fall of man.

Now if you want my authority for that let me give it to you again. The apostle Paul has put it all perfectly in a statement in Romans 8. He says, 'For the earnest expectation of the creature waiteth for the manifestation of the sons of God. For the creature was made subject to vanity, not willingly, but by reason of him who hath subjected the same in hope, because the creature itself also shall be delivered from the bondage of corruption into the glorious liberty of the children of God. For we know that the whole creation groaneth and travaileth in pain together until now.' 'Nature red in tooth and claw' is not nature as God made it. The whole of creation has suffered as the result of man's sin and as the result of man's fall, and we see nature struggling out of a corruption that it can never escape. That is what the apostle is saying.

So my argument is this – though it is not my argument, I am expounding the scriptures to you – God is not going to leave it like this. We have some great prophecies in the Old Testament about a day coming when the lion will lie down with the lamb, and the wolf with the ox and so on, and you know it is going to come. God cannot let the devil be supreme and victorious, so he is going to redeem the whole cosmos; not only individual man but the cosmos is going to be redeemed – everything is going to be delivered. The devil will not be allowed to be victorious. The Lord Jesus Christ came into this world, according to the apostle John, 'that he might destroy the works of the devil' (1 John 3:8) and he has come to do that and he is doing it and he is going to come back to make it complete.

Now let me give you some more verses which tell us this great and glorious thing which is held before us in the New Testament. Listen to our Lord himself putting it like this. Peter turned to our Lord one day and said, 'Behold, we have forsaken all, and followed thee; what shall we have therefore? And Jesus said unto them, Verily I say unto you, that ye which have followed me, in the regeneration when the son of man shall sit in the throne of his glory, ye also shall sit upon twelve thrones, judging the twelve tribes of Israel' – and so on. Read chapters twenty-four and twenty-five of Matthew's gospel where our Lord gives a great picture of the last things and you see it all.

And too, these Christian preachers, these apostles, the moment they began to preach, they began to say the same thing. Listen to Peter saying it. He had worked a miracle and the crowds came together and were ready to worship Peter and John. Peter said, 'Do not worship us, it is not us, it is this Jesus, the one you put to death. You crucified the prince of life! You did not realise what you were doing, you crucified the redeemer. Repent ye therefore, and be converted, that your sins may be blotted out, when the times of refreshing shall come from the presence of the Lord; and he shall send Jesus Christ, which before was preached unto you: whom the heaven must receive until the times of restitution of all things, which God hath spoken by the mouth of all his holy prophets since the world began.'

What does it mean? It means that he will come back in order to execute judgment. We have a great statement of that in the 2 Thessalonians 1. The son of God is going to come back to judge, he will judge the whole world in righteousness. And it is because one believes this that one is not put out by the present time. People ask – many Christians unfortunately – 'Is the Church coming to an end, is all finished, is the devil going to be supreme, is everything going to hell?' The answer is NO! it is God's purpose before the world began, and he will send his son to complete it. A Christian who is afraid of communism or any other 'ism' is not worthy of the name of Christian, he has forgotten 'that day' – the day of the manifestation of the son of God when he will come back to execute judgment and righteousness. Here it is again: 'And to you who are troubled rest with us, when the Lord Jesus shall be revealed from heaven with his mighty angels, in flaming fire taking vengeance on them that know not God, and that obey not the gospel of our Lord Jesus Christ: who shall be punished with everlasting destruction from the presence of the Lord, and from the glory of his power; when he shall come to be glorified in his saints'. There is a tremendous day coming! As once he came unknown, unobserved as the babe of Bethlehem, he will come again, and every eye shall see him, and it will be the last assize, the final judgment will be promulgated, and all his enemies, all the enemies of God, and all the clever men and women who have ridiculed the gospel and the way of salvation, all the clever men and women who have lived according to the lusts and the desires of the flesh and of the mind, all these will not only be condemned, they will be destroyed and will go to everlasting destruction from the presence of the Lord.

My dear friends, this is a tremendous statement. Do not look only at man's history, look at God's history, see how it has all been coming to pass, and this is as certain as everything that has ever happened. The great events of Revelation 20 are going to happen: 'And I saw a great white throne, and him that sat on it, from whose face the earth and the heaven fled away; and there was found no place for them. And I saw the dead, small and great, stand before God; and the books were opened; and another book was opened, which is the book of life: and the dead were judged out of those things which were written in the books, according to their works. And the sea gave up the dead which were in it; and death and hell delivered up the dead which were in them: and they were judged every man according to their works. And death and hell were cast into the lake of fire. This is the second death. And whosoever was not found written in the book of life was cast into the lake of fire.' That is what will happen! The devil and all his followers and forces, and all who have been deluded by him and who have believed his lie, are all going to be cast to that final destruction. That is what John is talking about. And Christ will purge the whole cosmos of every vestige and remnant of sin and evil. He is going to restore the universe to its pristine glory. 'There shall be a new heavens, and a new earth, wherein dwelleth righteousness.' That is the thing to hold on to. Not to try to identify the beasts of Revelation! Get hold of the big principle, my friend: new heavens, new earth, wherein dwelleth righteousness! He will set up his glorious kingdom. God's universe will be restored to its original condition as it was when he created it.

And this is the faith of the apostle Paul. He says, 'I am going to be there on that day, I am waiting for that.' That is the thing that enables him to say, 'nevertheless I am not ashamed'. Read again these magnificent words. All the scholars and authorities agree that 2 Timothy is the last letter the apostle ever wrote. Listen to him, then, as he faces the end; 'I am now ready to be offered, and the time of my departure' – the time of the striking of my tent – 'is at hand. I have fought a good fight, I have finished my course, I have kept the faith: henceforth there is laid up for me a crown of righteousness, which the Lord, the righteous judge, shall give me at that day: and not to me only, but unto all them also that love his appearing.' That day! In that day all who have believed in this Lord, this Saviour, all who have given themselves to him and have gone after him and are following him, will see him as he is, and they will be made like him, their very bodies will be glorified, and they will reign with him, and he will put a crown upon their heads. They will judge the world, they will judge angels, they will share in his everlasting and eternal glory.

Who is a Nero in the light of these things? A little Nero can put me to death but he cannot touch that. He can shorten my existence in this world, but he cannot detract even a second from the glory of eternity that is awaiting me. 'I am not troubled by this man,' says the apostle, 'and, Timothy, I am amazed at you and almost ashamed of you for being troubled yourself. What can this man do in the light of that day! He can do nothing. For in that day he will be cast to that lake of fire with the devil and all his forces and powers. He will be cast to the place to which he belongs and will spend his eternity in useless, endless remorse.' 'That day' – what is it? 'Well,' says Paul to the Romans, 'it is the day of "the manifestation of the sons of God". It is the day of "the glorious liberty of the children of God" – man appearing in all the glory of what God intended him to be in a glorified universe. No sorrow, no sin, no death, no tears, but joy unmixed and full of glory.'

Now, Paul keeps on talking about this. In writing to the Corinthians he says, 'For our light affliction, which is but for a moment, worketh for us a far more exceeding and eternal weight of glory'. That is what he is talking about – this 'weight of glory'. My dear friends, it transcends description. I do not know enough about it to tell you more. All I know is this, that God's universe is going to be restored, it is going to be delivered from everything that is evil and wrong. And it is his son who is going to do it! And if you and I are to enjoy that glory which is to come we must believe on him now. We must repent, we must see the folly and the error of our ways, we must get rid of this foolish pride of intellect and understanding that really understands nothing of these ultimate questions. We must become as little children, we must become as babies, we must become paupers. We must believe this 'form of sound words' of which the apostle is reminding Timothy. We must believe on the Lord Jesus Christ and the truth about him as Saviour and the one who ushers in this great salvation, including that great day that is to come. We must believe it whether we understand it or not. Just believe it and then you will begin to understand it, and you will be led on and on by the Spirit until your understanding makes you glory in it and you will be amazed at it. And though you may be thrown into prison and though everything may go against you, and hell may try to bring you down, you will be able to say, 'nevertheless I am not ashamed: for I know whom I have believed, and am persuaded [certain] that he is able to keep that which I have committed unto him against that day'. Oh, what a day! Have you ever had a glimpse of it, have you ever thought about it? Let me try to give you one glimpse by quoting some words of Henry Alford:

> Ten thousand times ten thousand,
> In sparkling raiment bright;
> The armies of the ransomed saints
> Throng up the steeps of light;
> 'Tis finished! all is finished,
> Their fight with death and sin;
> Fling open wide the golden gates,
> And let the victors in.

What rush of hallelujahs
Fills all the earth and sky;
What ringing of a thousand harps
Bespeaks the triumph nigh!
O day, for which creation
And all its tribes were made;
O joy, for all its former woes
A thousandfold repaid!

Bring near thy great salvation
Thou lamb for sinners slain;
Fill up the roll of thine elect,
Then take thy power and reign;
Appear, desire of nations;
Thine exiles long for home;
Show in the heavens thy promised sign:
Thou prince and Saviour, come!

Even so, come, Lord Jesus, and reign. Amen.

Chapter Eleven

SUNDAY EVENING SERMON
21st June 1964

Persuaded

For the which cause I also suffer these things: nevertheless I am not ashamed: for I know whom I have believed, and am persuaded that he is able to keep that which I have committed unto him against that day (2 Tim. 1:12).

We must look once more at this tremendous statement, because there is still one great and important aspect of this matter that we have not considered, and that is the application.

We have here, as I have been trying to show, this magnificent challenge, if you like, of the Christian gospel, the message that comes to us as an offer and a challenge. The gospel is always challenging us and our view of life and our way of living, and then it comes as an offer to us, and there it is, all summarised in this very wonderful verse in which the great apostle simply states his experience. What Paul is really saying, as we have seen, is that there is only one thing that can enable a man to be joyful even in a prison, and even to look into the face of death with a smile and a spirit of rejoicing, and that is this gospel. Well now, that obviously implies certain other things. How are we to get into this position? Are we there at this moment? How are you standing up to life, how are you getting on in this world? Do you ever contemplate old age? Do you ever contemplate death? Do you ever contemplate the death of those who are dear to you? Do you ever contemplate the loss of your health? What are you living on?

You say, 'I am very happy at the moment, I never had it so good.' All right, let us imagine that things go wrong, you lose your health, you lose your jobs, a war comes, bombs are set off . . . what then? Now that is the question, and the challenge is, you see, are we in a position tonight to be able to say, 'I do not care what happens, my position will remain exactly the same'?

But how do we come to that? The answer, according to the apostle, is that we have got to hold on to these things, the things of which he is reminding Timothy, and we can only get into this position if we carry out the instructions that Paul gave to this young follower and disciple of his, this young minister Timothy. What have we got to do? Essentially, it is simple. The whole position of the apostle depended upon the Lord Jesus Christ. He kept on saying that. He was constantly using the name, showing him to Timothy. Of course, if you know anything at all about the New Testament, you must know that what changed Paul, and the whole course of his life, was his meeting with the Lord Jesus Christ on the road to Damascus: the brilliant Pharisee, the expert in the legalisms and the minutiæ of the Jewish law suddenly became a preacher of the gospel that he had reviled and persecuted. It is one of the great stories of all history, it is one of the most dramatic changes that has ever taken place in a man's life.

What changed him? There is only one answer, it is the Lord Jesus Christ: and, of course, Christianity is 'the Lord Jesus Christ'. That is the one test of the Christian faith. There are people who are talking about Christianity today who never mention this name at all. What they have really got is a philosophy that may use certain of the terms but which is not related to the person. According to Paul's teaching, this person is the alpha and the omega, the first and the last, the beginning and the end, he is the all, and in all, and without him there is nothing. He is everything.

Now, the apostle tells us that to get into the position that he is in, there are certain things that are imperative, absolute essentials. The first is, we must believe the message concerning this person, the Lord Jesus Christ. 'I know whom I have believed.' Now, I have said that we are in the realm of practical application, and I know no more fundamentally vital questions than these very ones that I am going to put to you now as simply as I can. I have tried to take you through the elements of the Christian faith, the elements of Christian doctrine – they are all here, this is a most marvellous summary of essential Christian doctrines, and we have looked at them one by one. But, it has all been a waste of time and energy unless they have become a practical reality in your life. A preacher who does not apply his message is not worth his salt, he is a lecturer. Preaching always means application, and however much I may have held the doctrines before you, they will not help you unless you know something about these particular points which the apostle enumerates here.

Well, the first is, I say again, that we must believe in this person. At a communion service, we have a table in front of us with bread and wine upon it – what does all that mean? Why do we do this? Is it some strange ritual that we are just perpetuating because we have not the sense to stop doing it? Is it some pagan rite? What is this bread, this wine? Well, what it does is to bring us back immediately to history, and it brings us back to this blessed person, Jesus Christ, the one who, while having that last supper with his disciples, took bread and broke it, and then poured out wine into a vessel. This is history, he did it the night when he was betrayed. You see, we are concerned now about a person, and this is how the Bible, and the New Testament in particular, deals with and solves this problem of life and living. As we have seen, it does not start with the problem, it takes us away back to something that lies at the back of everything. Oh, the world, of course, approaches the problem politically and socially, psychologically, or by means of the cults, which are just psychological tricks, and so on. That is how the world does it, it is always starting with the problem and trying to do something about that. The Bible does not do that; the Bible says, look – begin here, with Jesus Christ, Jesus of Nazareth, this person . . .

In other words the teaching is that this person is the key to history, that we really do not understand anything truly, apart from him, and that the most momentous and cataclysmic event that has ever taken place in the whole history of the world is the birth of a baby in a stable in Bethlehem, the one who was put in the manger and whom they called Jesus. Jesus of Nazareth. Who is he? Now, the centre of Paul's universe was that Jesus of Nazareth was the son of God, that he had come out of eternity into time. 'The word was made flesh, and dwelt among us.' The incarnation! That God hath visited and redeemed his people. We have seen how, at a given point in history, because the world was in a muddle, because it was a place of sin and of shame, because it was sinful and rebellious, because it was going to pieces and going to destruction, 'when the fulness of the time was come, God sent forth his son, made of a woman, made under the law, to redeem them that were under the law'. What we must believe is that God has done something about this world, that we are not left to ourselves, we are not left to civilisation, we are not left to learning, we are not left to political action. God has done the vital thing, the only thing that can save us, and he has done it by sending his only son into the world.

Now this is the hub of everything: 'Believe on the Lord Jesus Christ', the New Testament keeps on saying. You remember the Philippian jailor, desperate fellow? He had got two extraordinary prisoners, Paul and Silas. These men were in the innermost prison with their feet fast in the stocks but at midnight they were singing, they were praying and singing praises unto God. Then there was an earthquake and the jailor thought that all the prisoners had escaped, 'But Paul cried with a loud voice, saying, Do thyself no harm:' – he was about to commit suicide, thinking he was going to get into trouble for allowing the prisoners to escape – 'Do thyself no harm: for we are all here'. The man was astonished and he came trembling, and he looked at these two strange prisoners, the like of whom he had never seen before, and he said, 'Sirs, what must I do to be saved?' And there was only one answer to give him; Paul told him what he told Timothy, 'Believe on the Lord Jesus Christ, and thou shalt be saved, and thy house'; believe that Jesus of Nazareth is the son of God, that

God has entered into the problem of man and has done something in this person, which is the only solution. So you look at the person and you must believe that Jesus of Nazareth, the one who worked as a carpenter until the age of thirty, and then began to preach in that astounding manner and to work miracles, is the eternal son of God.

Now, this is shattering, is it not? this is tremendous. You see, we think in terms of men, and we are rightly interested in history and we rightly pay homage to great men, and we read their works and are edified by them; but none of them can solve the problem, all of them were failures themselves. Though they stand on tiptoe and on one another's shoulders they are not big enough. But here is someone who has come down from heaven, who is unique, who stands alone. He is God as well as man. This is the whole doctrine of the incarnation. The person of Christ, two natures in one person.

And then think again of what he did. What was he doing in this world? Well, let him answer. 'The son of man' he said, 'is come to seek and to save that which was lost.' That is what he was doing here. A man had been listening to him one day and he thought, 'Well, this is a very able man, this is the very man I have been looking for to advise me. I have got this dispute with my brother about the inheritance.' So he put his question to our Lord and he said, 'Master, speak to my brother that he divide the inheritance with me', and our Lord turned on him and said, 'Man, who made me a judge or a divider over you?' Do you think I have come into this world to settle disputes like that? No! 'The son of man is come to seek and to save that which was lost.' 'The son of man', he says again, 'came not to be ministered unto, but to minister, and to give his life a ransom for many.'

What does all this mean? Ah, look at him again; listen to him, listen to his teaching. Do you think that he came into this world simply to give us the highest ethical and moral teaching that the world has ever known? Well you know the answer to that is, that the Greek philosophers had come very near this, though they had failed. He did not come merely to teach, and there is a very good reason for that. If he had come only to teach, then of all persons who have ever been in this world, he would have damned us more than anybody else. How easy it is to talk about living the sermon on the mount! Have you ever tried it? How easy to talk about keeping the ten commandments! Have we ever done so? Remember they include the expression 'Thou shalt not covet'. You must not sin even in your imagination, leave alone in actions. No, he did teach but he did not come to teach. 'He steadfastly set his face to go to Jerusalem.' When his own friends were pleading with him not to go there he said, 'I must'! He had come for that. There was an 'hour' in his life and he had come for this climactic hour.

What is this hour? Oh, it is the hour of his death! The whole teaching of the New Testament is that the son of God came into this world in order to die. Why? Because it was the only way whereby he could deliver us, whereby he could take the punishment of our sins upon himself and thereby reconcile us to God, or, to put it another way, God was reconciling us unto himself by punishing our sins in his son whom he had sent to bear them. That is the essence of the New Testament teaching: bread broken, poured out wine, blood shed! This is the very essence of the gospel. 'Who hath saved us . . . not according to our works, but according to his own purpose and grace, which was given us in Christ Jesus before the world began, but is now made manifest by the appearing of our Saviour Jesus Christ, who hath abolished death, and hath brought life and immortality to light through the gospel.'

So then, exactly what does 'Believe on the Lord Jesus Christ' mean? It means that we must believe this record that Jesus of Nazareth is the only begotten son of God – God and man – and that he came into this world to bear the punishment of our sins himself, in order that you and I might be forgiven and might become the sons and the children of God. Believe! We must believe that record. There is no salvation apart from that. There is no experience such as Paul had apart from that. The whole of Paul's position, I repeat, depends upon the fact which he only discovered on the road to Damascus – that the Jesus whom he had reviled and blasphemed and persecuted as but a carpenter, this 'fellow' whom he and all the other Pharisees abominated, is none other than the Lord of glory, the Lord from heaven, the very son of God. As he puts it to the Galatians, 'The son of God, who loved me, and gave himself for me'. That is believing. There is the first step. 'I know whom I have believed.'

But you notice there is a second element here, and we must go on because the first is not enough. We must not only believe these things about him, we must be *persuaded* of them. 'Nevertheless I am not ashamed', because I have been persuaded. 'I know whom I have believed, and am persuaded that he is able to keep that which I have committed unto him against that day.' He has been persuaded of these things, and of course this is a very essential element. Oh, this terrible distinction, and what a vital distinction it is, between knowing about things and being persuaded of them; knowing things intellectually, knowing things with a kind of intellectual apprehension, and really being persuaded of them.

I imagine that the best way, perhaps, of putting the difference is this; that as long as your understanding is merely intellectual, you are more or less looking on at it all in a detached manner. You say, 'Yes, I have read the evidence, I have read the Bible, I have read books on the Bible, I have considered it all; I am of the opinion that this statement concerning him is right,' and so on. But you are doing it like a judge on the bench and you are quite detached, you are not involved. That is not saving faith. That is intellectual belief, and that does not change anybody. It is essential, you have got to start with it, but you must not stop at it. Having realised what the truth is, having realised that Christianity does not just mean doing good and being better than certain obvious profligate sinners who are in the gutters – having realised that this Jesus, this person, is essential and central, and having come to terms with the truth concerning him, you go on to this next step, that these truths have become real to you, that they have affected you, that you begin to feel their power; that you are no longer in the detached position of the spectator, as it were, who is looking on.

We have all been guilty of this detached position, it is

instinctive in man, it is something which is quite natural. We read the books and our attitude is, 'Yes, I know the case for Mohammedanism, I know the case for Hinduism, I know the case for Confucianism, and I know the case for Christianity, and I have got it all at my fingertips.' Oh, if that is your position, if you are looking down on this, you are outside it. To be persuaded means that it comes to you with power, that you realise that it is talking to you personally, that it is saying to you the most momentous thing you have ever heard in your life, or ever can hear, that it has made you really concerned about yourself. I know that when we get into trouble, when we do wrong and then suffer remorse, we say, 'Well, of course, my religion perhaps can help me at this point, I want to get rid of my pain.' But now you get beyond all that, you begin to see yourself in the context of eternity and you say, 'I now see and believe that this Jesus of Nazareth came into the world, and died on the cross,' and you suddenly see the truth and say, 'Well, of course, I am involved in that, he came for me.' The truth becomes personal.

I think I have told this story before, it illustrates perfectly the way in which so many stumble at this personal aspect of religion. They do not object to Christianity as long as it is represented as a merely moral, ethical system and teaching; and, indeed, they do not object to marvellous statements about the son of God; they like paintings that tend to express it all, and sculpture and architecture and so on. They think it is very wonderful and a noble idea, but the moment it becomes personal they object to it. As Lord Melbourne, the first Prime Minister of Queen Victoria, said, on leaving the church where he had heard a very searching sermon, they say, 'Things are coming to a pretty pass if religion is going to start being personal.' Ah, it is one thing to be interested in theology, but if it becomes personal . . . !

So I say it must be: 'I have been persuaded,' and Paul was persuaded, and persuaded to the extent that it revolutionised his life and he became the object of scorn and of persecution on the part of the very people who had revered him and had honoured him above all others as a teacher. Very well then, this is the second thing, that we are not only aware of the statements, but that we have been persuaded of them, that we realise their relevance to us and that we are involved in all that they say.

But even that does not finish the matter nor exhaust it. The next step, said the apostle, was that he was so persuaded of the truth that he committed himself to it. 'I know whom I have believed, and am persuaded that he is able to keep that which I have committed unto him' or 'that he is able to guard' if you like (I say this for the sake of the pundits) 'my deposit'. But these old Authorised translators were giving us the sense and the meaning. What is my 'deposit'? It is something that I put into the bank, into the deposit account, or into some post office account; I make my deposit, that which I have committed to their safe keeping. It is safe, 'that which I have committed unto him'.

And this is again an absolutely vital and essential part of saving faith. It is the thing that differentiates saving faith from a mere intellectual belief. It is this idea that you 'commit' yourself to him. You see you are no longer taking a theoretical, academic interest in him, you have come to see now that his coming into this world is because of what *you* are; not the world, but you, because you are a part of the world, and the world means nothing but a collection of people like you, who have come now to this personal position. And now you have seen it so plainly, you have seen its vital truth so clearly, that you have committed yourself and your soul and its eternal safe keeping to him.

I suppose there is nothing that is more essential to the peace and the rest and the quiet that the apostle was so obviously enjoying than this very element of committal, for there is nothing that can make a man so unhappy and so restless, so frightened of life and so frightened of death in particular, as that a man should be trying to reconcile himself to God: there is nothing more fearful than that. You see, you have been awakened out of your slumber. At one time you would have said, 'Well, as long as I am a decent fellow nothing else matters very much, and in any case I am very much better than the majority of people I see round and about me. I do not live for the things they live for, I have never got drunk, I have never committed adultery, I am all right . . .'

Well, you have been awakened out of that sort of nonsense, that childish nonsense, and you have come to realise that there is a God whom you have got to meet, that you are a man and not a machine, and that God made man in his own image and stamped something of his own eternal being upon you, and that he holds you responsible. He pays you the compliment of saying, 'You are a man and not an animal and a beast, and I demand of you the living and the life of a man.' When you have come to realise that, you have realised with the apostle Paul that all your supposed righteousness is but dung and loss and refuse, and that all your righteousness is but as 'filthy rags'. And here you are, you begin to realise what you are as a man; and you are aware of the great God who has made you and who is going to be your judge at the end, and you say, 'What can I do, the time is short, I must live a better life.' So you start on it and you find you cannot do it, and you become more conscious of your failures and of all your blemishes. Those who say this more and more are for the most part those who have been conscious of their failure; they are those who can say from experience,

> Not the labours of my hands
> Can fulfil Thy law's demands;
> Could my zeal no respite know,
> Could my tears for ever flow,
> All for sin could not atone.

The greatest agony a person, a soul, can ever know, is the agony of trying to reconcile himself unto God. You see the days slipping by, you see death and eternity and the judgment coming nearer and you are aware of all this evil, this wrongness, within, indeed, that your very nature is wrong. The trouble is, you say, 'not that I do things that are wrong, but that I should even want to do them, what is this in me . . . Oh, this vile body, this other law in my members dragging me down, this conflict within me, this dualism that is in me, how can I get rid of it. O wretched man that I am! who shall deliver me?' And you are completely and utterly hopeless; and in that state, of course, there is nothing that is more terrifying than death, because any man who is awakened to the reality of his soul and to God, knows that there is nothing more terrible than death. Why? Because it means the end of our period of probation and of trial and of opportunity. Our Lord himself talked about the great gulf that is fixed between heaven and hell and that there is no passing from one to the other beyond death. People talk about a second chance. Where do they get their authority for it? There is none. What the Bible says is that a man decides his eternal state and destiny in this world, and his time is short. 'I see God and I see myself,' he says, 'what can I do? I cannot taste death with tranquillity and with calm and with peace: it is impossible. Death is my last enemy and I do everything I can to avoid it and to postpone it. But, you see, I need more time, I need more opportunity, and yet, I know that all the extra time will avail me nothing, because I am wrong and I cannot erase my past sins. I cannot claim the love of God because I have rebelled against him, I have dismissed him, I have blasphemed him, and I deserve nothing from him but punishment.'

Now while a man is in that condition he is intensely unhappy and miserable, failing in life and afraid of death. This is the way of escape, says the apostle; you must not only believe the facts concerning the person of Jesus of Nazareth, you must not only believe as a kind of wonderful picture or theory or idea that he died for you. You have got to go beyond that; you have got to come to the point in which you say,

> I lay my sins on Jesus,
> The spotless lamb of God.

You come to him in your utter desperation and say,

> Just as I am, without one plea
> But that thy blood was shed for me,
> And that thou bid'st me come to thee,
> O lamb of God, I come.

You say this which has been said in so many different ways by some of the greatest Christian poets (I have already quoted from this hymn):

> Rock of ages, cleft for me,
> Let me hide myself in thee;
> Let the water and the blood,
> From thy riven side which flowed,
> Be of sin the double cure,
> Cleanse me from its guilt and power.

> Not the labours of my hands
> Can fulfil thy law's demands;
> Could my zeal no respite know,
> Could my tears for ever flow,
> All for sin could not atone;

But then you go on to the last line:

> Thou must save, and thou alone.

Then you go to him and say:

> Nothing in my hand I bring;
> Simply to thy cross I cling;

That is the committal – 'I cling'!

> Naked, come to thee for dress;
> Helpless, look to thee for grace;
> Foul, I to the fountain fly;
> Wash me, Saviour, or I die.

That is the committal, and this is the most tremendous thing that can ever happen to a man. This is the only way in which you will ever find peace, this is the only way in which you will ever really get rid of the fear of death, this is the only way in which you will ever be able to master life. You take your soul, as it is in its rags and tatters, its filth and all the mud and the mire of evil that is upon it, and you hand it over to him, like a man who puts a treasure, or his money, in a safe deposit. You just take yourself as you are, and put yourself in his hands, you stop thinking about your soul, you stop worrying about your soul. The devil will come and say, 'Who are you?' The world will point its finger. You say, 'Don't bother me,' and you turn to God and say:

> Be thou my shield and hiding-place
> That sheltered near thy side,
> I may my fierce accuser face
> And tell him, thou hast died.

And you find peace and rest.

You can prove you are persuaded. You hand your case entirely over to him: 'I lay my sins on Jesus'. That is the committal. I am committed. I am no longer worrying. I have often used this illustration to help people who are harassed by the devil. They come to me and they say, 'You know, I believe and yet I am troubled, I am not happy; I don't know . . .' Then I say to them, 'Why will you go on listening to the devil?' How can they stop doing that? I sometimes have used this very simple illustration, so I repeat it to you because it helps me and I find it helps them. I put it like this.

Let us imagine, I say, that you are going for a holiday and that you have got some possession which, though not valuable in itself, is of great value to you. It has certain personal associations and it is the one thing in all your possessions that you never want to lose, and you never want to be robbed of it. But you want to go on holiday and you cannot take this thing with you, so you come to me and say, 'I wonder whether you would be good enough to look after this while I am away. Are you going to be home for the next three weeks?' I tell you that I am and that I will be delighted to take care of it. 'You go away on your holiday,' I say, 'and forget all about it, leave it with me.' 'Right,' you say, 'thank you very much,' and off you go delighted. And there am I in my study reading or writing, and in about an hour's time my telephone goes. I take it up, and ask, 'Who is there?' You are on the line. 'What do you want?' I say. 'Is that thing I left with you all right?' you ask anxiously.

Yes, I hope this amuses you, because I hope it will sink in that you are laughing at yourself spiritually. You laugh at a person who would do that, do you not, with this human material deposit. You see, people go on doing that. Another couple of hours perhaps, and the telephone goes again: 'Who is there?' – 'Is that thing I left with you still all right?' And in the end I say, 'Look here, do you trust me or do you not? If you have left that thing in my safe keeping, if you have deposited it with me, you are insulting me. Get on and enjoy your holiday; you must stop thinking about this. If you go on like that you are insulting me, you are not trusting me.' 'That which I have committed unto him against that day.' 'I am not worried,' says Paul, 'I am not frightened of death, I am not frightened of life or death or anything; I have committed it to him and I do not think about it. It is in his keeping, not in mine.' That is the committal part of faith and it is an absolute essential. If you, at any point, take back again to yourself any part of your salvation you are insulting him and you are going to make yourself miserable. We become miserable as Christians only when we fall back upon our own works and our own efforts and our own endeavours. Very well, it means committal – belief, persuasion, committal.

Then, it has certain implications and these are absolutely vital. For one thing, it means that our whole life will now be controlled by him. If you want the experience of the apostle you must live like the apostle. There is another vital distinction. You remember what one of the old Puritans said about that man Balaam in the Old Testament? Balaam said, 'Let me die the death of the righteous, and let my last end be like his'.

What was the matter with Balaam? The old Puritan was a profound psychologist, he said, 'Balaam wanted to die like the righteous but he did not want to live like the righteous,' and if you do not live like the righteous, you will not die like the righteous. There are no short cuts in the spiritual life. We cannot play fast and loose with God. We cannot extract just what we want and leave the rest. It is all or nothing in this Christian life.

Now, Paul says that a man who really has believed and has committed himself is a man whose whole life is now controlled by the Lord Jesus Christ. He is everywhere, he dominates the whole life, he is the beginning and the end, the centre and the circumference. How does this show itself? Paul maintains that this Lord, and the truth about him, determines a man's entire view of life in this world, and there is nothing more wonderful than this. Some people seem to think that Christianity is a message which says, 'Come to Jesus, believe in him and you will live happily ever afterwards.' It is an absolute travesty of the gospel, it is a complete lie.

There is no view in the world today that is so realistic about life in this world as the Christian Gospel, and there is nothing about it that I glory in more, than that the gospel has delivered me from the false optimism of the non-Christian. The non-Christian, poor fellow, is always hoping that the world is going to become a perfect place. He believes that if he only organises political and social and other actions he really can get a perfect world. Oh, the poor, benighted, deluded souls! That is why they are so unhappy, they are always straining after the impossible. The gospel delivers us from all that at the very beginning. The gospel tells us, as nothing else tells us, that this is a very evil world. This apostle, in writing to the Galatians, calls it 'this present evil world'. The Bible view of it, from one standpoint, is the most pessimistic view possible; that is, if we just look at life as it is. It is everybody else who thinks that the world can be put right. The Bible says it cannot, it is so hopeless that the son of God had to come into it to do something about it, and he will have to come into it again.

So the Bible gives me great release and ease and peace at the very beginning. It says, 'Do not paint rosy pictures of life in this world, do not put on those rose-tinted spectacles, do not be deluded by the poets in certain moods or by the glib optimism of the Victorians and by that false idealism. You have got to see life steadily, you have got to see it whole, you have got to see it realistically, and the moment you do that, you will expect nothing from it but what you are getting, and it might get worse.'

Now, the apostle says all this to Timothy. Timothy was in trouble because he had not realised that. Paul tells him in that second chapter: 'Thou therefore endure hardness, as a good soldier of Jesus Christ. No man that warreth entangleth himself with the affairs of this life; that he may please him who hath chosen him to be a soldier' – and so on. He says, 'I suffer trouble, even as an evil doer, even unto bonds . . . Therefore I endure all things . . .' The biblical view is just that, and our Lord said the same thing: 'In the world ye shall have tribulations'. That is what the son of God said. He did not say, 'Believe in me and enter into a magic place, into some kind of Elysium, and you will never have another trouble.' He says, 'No, in the world ye shall have tribulations'. So when they come, the Christian is not surprised, his world is not shattered. He says, 'I am living in a world that rejected the son of God when he came into it: "He came unto his own, and his own received him not"'. That is the sort of world I am living in, I don't expect men to live decently and in order, I expect nothing but what I am seeing. Man is the slave of sin and of Satan, therefore he lives according to that whole position, and I am not surprised. I am not surprised at world wars, I am not surprised at atomic and hydrogen bombs, I am not surprised at adultery and lust, I am not surprised at theft and robbery, I am not surprised at juvenile delinquency and all the present moral muddle. I am not surprised, I expect it, I anticipate it, and if the world should turn against Christians and massacre us, I shall not be surprised. There is nothing too bad for man in sin. "I was born in sin, and shaped in iniquity" myself, and I know the plague of my own heart. I tremble to think what I might have been but for the grace of God. I am far from perfect, but oh, what I might have been! "I am what I am by the grace of God"! and I was so vile that nothing but the grace of God could lift me up out of it.'

Very well then, the whole of a man's view of life is entirely changed immediately he becomes a Christian. But secondly – and do notice this – this man who has believed on the Lord Jesus Christ, and committed himself to him, is a man who is prepared to suffer anything rather than deny him. Have you noticed this wonderful phrase as we have been considering this great passage: Paul says to Timothy, 'Be not thou therefore ashamed of the testimony of our Lord, nor of me his prisoner . . .' Paul does not describe himself as the prisoner of the Emperor Nero, which in actual fact he was, for that is not how he sees it. He says, 'I am a prisoner of the Lord Jesus Christ' – 'His prisoner'. And then he says in the twelfth verse, 'For the which cause' – 'it is because I am a preacher and an apostle, and a teacher of the Gentiles' – it is for this cause that I also suffer these things. I am in prison. Why? Because I am a Christian, because I am preaching the gospel.

What he is saying, you see, is this: 'The authorities have told me that if I go on preaching this gospel I shall stay in prison; but that if I stop preaching it, I shall be set free. If I will only say "Caesar is Lord" instead of saying that "Jesus is Lord" I will get my liberty. Why don't I say it? I cannot say that' says Paul. 'I have believed in him, I have committed my soul to him. He is the son of God, he is my Saviour, I will go to death rather than deny him. Deny him? The thing is unthinkable. Death is nothing. Oh no,' says Paul, 'the whole of my life is determined and controlled by him.' And to Timothy he says, 'Be not thou therefore ashamed of the testimony of our Lord, nor of me his prisoner: but be thou partaker of the afflictions of the gospel according to the power of God'. God will give you power to bear them. 'But,' he says, 'you must be so dominated by this, that you will not be frightened when they threaten you. They are saying, "We have put your master into prison, we will put you in too," and you are frightened and alarmed and you are beginning to wonder.

Man,' says Paul, 'hold on; look again at what you believe, hold on to that. What can they do when you are in his hands? It is nothing! He dominates the whole of life, and a Christian would sooner lose everything, his life included, rather than deny this Lord in whom he has believed.'

Indeed, belief in the Lord Jesus Christ goes further: it enables the Christian to glory even in tribulations. The apostle is never tired of saying that. You remember how he puts it in writing to the Romans in chapter five? He says, 'Therefore being justified by faith, we have peace with God . . . by whom also we have access by faith into this grace wherein we stand, and rejoice in hope of the glory of God.' But go on! 'And not only so, but we glory in tribulations also: knowing that tribulation worketh patience; and patience, experience; and experience, hope: and hope maketh not ashamed; because the love of God is shed abroad in our hearts by the Holy Ghost which is given unto us.' He rejoices in tribulations. Why?

Well, for this reason: the more he gets of tribulations and trials, and the more he suffers persecutions and imprisonments, the more is he driven to realise that his soul is in the safe keeping of that blessed Lord; the more the world reviles him, the more it drives him to his Lord and master. The testimony of the saints throughout the centuries is universal on this one point – that times of persecution have been the most glorious times they ever experienced, because, when everything was going well they tended to forget their Lord; but when things went wrong and they were bereft of all their pleasures and enjoyments and they were left with nothing in the world, then they were driven back to him, and they were drawn closer to him and they experienced his smile and his power. 'For our light affliction,' says Paul to the Corinthians, 'which is but for a moment, worketh for us a far more exceeding and eternal weight of glory; While we look not at the things which are seen, but at the things which are not seen: for the things which are seen are temporal; but the things which are not seen are eternal.' So, the Christian is a man who believes in the Lord Jesus Christ, he is persuaded concerning him, he commits himself to him, his life is dominated by him.

And, lastly, he is a man who has absolute unshakeable confidence in him. 'Nevertheless I am not ashamed.' Why? Well, because 'I know whom I have believed, and am persuaded that he is able' – able! – 'to keep that which I have committed unto him against that day'. I know him, and because I know him, I know something about him, and I know what is true of him. What is it? Oh, this is the final confidence of the Christian: put him into prison, throw him to the lions in the arena, do what you like to him, it does not matter, he knows whom he has believed. What does he know about him?

Oh! think of these things, and spend the rest of your time on earth in contemplating them and you will do so in eternity. His love. His love! How do I know about his love? I know about his love because he went to the cross on Calvary's hill in my stead. His body was broken, his blood was shed for me. 'The Son of God, who loved me, and gave himself for me.' The blaspheming Pharisee, Saul of Tarsus, saw him on the road to Damascus, and this is what broke his heart: that he realised that that Lord whom he had reviled and blasphemed and persecuted was loving him even while he was doing that to his name. 'The son of God who loved *me*, and gave himself for *me*.' And if he died for me, then he will do anything for me. He so loved me that he gave his life for me. That is what I know for certain about him. I know that that is his relationship to me. He came into this world, he left the glory of heaven because he loved me; he suffered the contradiction of sinners against himself while he was here – for me. He trod the winepress alone – for me. He was nailed to the tree – for me. He had done no wrong, they could not find any harm in him, he was guiltless, apart from sinners. But he died and was buried in a grave! Oh, I have no doubt about his love! That is why I can leave my deposit with him, I know indeed that he loves me in a way that I will never understand. I think I know something about it, but I know so little, 'I know in part, and I understand in part'. My knowledge, oh, how puny it is! His love to me! The height, the depth, the length, the breadth; to know the love of Christ, which passeth knowledge. But I know enough to trust him. He has given me such absolute proof of it on the cross.

And then I have his promises. I am not afraid of life. Why not? Because he has said, 'I will never leave thee, nor forsake thee.' Never! He has promised, he has pledged to keep me, to lead me all the way, and to bring me into the glory everlasting.

What else? Well, he has made another tremendous promise: 'Let not your heart be troubled: ye believe in God, believe also in me. In my father's house are many mansions: if it were not so, I would have told you. I go to prepare a place for you. And if I go and prepare a place for you, I will come again, and receive you unto myself; that where I am, there ye may be also.' Who is Nero! What are these little officials? What is the world and hell? He has gone to prepare a place for me, and he will come again. It is his promise. And his promises are ever sure.

Which brings me to the third thing – his constancy. The apostle puts this in a very striking form in the second chapter of this epistle to Timothy. He says, 'It is a faithful saying: For if we be dead with him, we shall also live with him: if we suffer, we shall also reign with him: if we deny him, he also will deny us: if we believe not, yet he abideth faithful'. But more – 'he cannot deny himself'. Thank God for it! He cannot deny himself. We are inconstant, we are changeable, he is unchangeable. His character is unchangeable. 'Jesus Christ, the same yesterday, today, and for ever.' He cannot change! this is the anchor of my soul, that he cannot change. I can – he cannot. His word is true, his constancy is absolute. So that at my worst moments I can say this:

When darkness seems to hide his face
I rest on his unchanging grace;
In every high and stormy gale
My anchor holds within the veil;
On Christ the solid rock I stand
All other ground is sinking sand.

I know his love, I know his promises, I know his constancy,

and I know his ability and his power. Someone may come to me and say, 'That's all very well, I am ready for you to say that Jesus of Nazareth was very wonderful, but he is dead and gone and you are still in this world, and life is vile and evil and vicious, and death is coming and all these things . . . Are you all right?' I am! 'He is *able* – "to keep that which I have committed unto him".' 'How do you know that?' says someone. Well, I know it because he has already 'abolished death' and has brought 'life and immortality to light'. You see, what I know about him is this – that he was in this world and that the world then was exactly as the world is now. I know that he 'was tempted in all points like as we are, yet without sin'; I know that the devil came in person to tempt him and still could not get him down. I mean that the devil marshalled all his forces and still Christ defeated him. He drove out devils, he mastered every evil power, there was nothing he could not do.

And then the devil produced his trump card. The devil had the power over death and he brought him to death, thinking that thereby he had finally defeated him. But we know what happened – the resurrection! He has undone death, he has disannulled death, he has smashed it, he has burst asunder the bands of death and risen triumphant o'er the grave. He has brought life and immortality to light! The last enemy has been conquered! There is nothing he has not conquered. 'He is able'! 'I am persuaded, that neither death, nor life, nor angels, nor principalities, nor powers, nor things present, nor things to come, nor height, nor depth, nor any other creature, shall be able to separate us from the love of God, which is in Christ Jesus our Lord.'

My dear friends, I leave you with a question: have you been persuaded? Have you been persuaded about these things? As you are in the midst of life, have you been persuaded of these things? Have you been persuaded about him, who he is, what he has done? Are you sure about these things? Have you trusted him, have you given yourself to him, have you committed your whole eternal future to him? Is he mastering and dominating your life? Are you relying upon him and the power of his might? Is that your position? Have you been persuaded? Listen to him again: listen to him as he says, 'I am come that they might have life, and that they might have it more abundantly'. 'I am come to seek and to save that which is lost.' Listen to him!

But is it true? Well, listen to those who have believed him, listen to those who have been persuaded by him, listen to those who have committed themselves to him and who rely upon him; listen to this man Paul, listen to all the other apostles, listen to those unknown people who were thrown to the lions in the arena in Rome and so many other places; listen to those men whose graves are still there to be seen in those places just outside Rome; listen to the martyrs, to the confessors, to the Reformers, listen to the Covenanters, listen to God's people throughout the ages, and they will all say the same thing to you. 'He is able!' He is willing! Doubt no more. Have you been persuaded?

> Art thou weary, art thou languid,
> Art thou sore distressed?
> 'Come to me,' saith one, 'and coming,
> Be at rest.'

> Hath he marks to lead me to him,
> If he be my guide?

'Yes!' is the answer:

> In his feet and hands are wound-prints,
> And his side.

> Is there diadem, as monarch,
> That his brow adorns?

Will I find him in palaces, or amongst the great and the mighty?

Yea, a crown, in very surety,
But of thorns.

If I find him, if I follow,
What his guerdon here?

Is it going to be 'they all lived happily ever afterwards'? Is it
that I am carried on a bed of roses in some celestial train to
heaven? No, no!

Many a sorrow, many a labour,
Many a tear.

If I still hold closely to him
What hath he at last?

That is the question – 'at last' –

Sorrow vanquished, labour ended,
Jordan past.

He has taken the sting out of death. 'For me to live is Christ,
and to die is gain.' 'Jordan past!'

If I ask him to receive me,
Will he say me nay?

Will he remind me of all the sins I have ever committed?
Will he remind me of the vileness of my heart? 'If I ask him to
receive me, Will he say me nay?'

Not till earth and not till heaven
Pass away.

Finding, following keeping, struggling,
Is he sure to bless?

Listen!

Saints, apostles, prophets, martyrs,
Answer, 'Yes!'

Oh, that you might hear that 'Yes'! He himself has spoken
to you: 'Come unto me,' he says. But listen to these witnesses
through the running centuries: 'Saints, apostles, prophets';
the martyr at the stake, the men who died in Smithfield or in
Oxford, or wherever else they may have died – go and ask
them. 'Saints, apostles, prophets, martyrs, Answer' – Oh,
that I could utter that word 'Yes'! What would I not give if I
could but conduct this amazing choir of saints, apostles,
prophets, martyrs. Here they are, this great heavenly choir,
the sopranos, the altos, the tenors, the basses – I see them
there. 'What is your answer?' I ask. Can you hear it? 'Saints,
apostles, prophets, martyrs, answer, "Yes".' Yes! 'Trust
him,' they say. Trust him! Commit your soul to him! He will
receive you and he will keep you.

From him that loves me now so well
What power my soul can sever?
Shall life? or death? or earth? or hell?
No! I am his for ever.

Be persuaded, my dear friend, and commit your soul and
your eternal welfare to him, and then whatever may happen
to you in this life and in this world you will always be able to
say: 'Nevertheless I am not ashamed: for I know whom I have
believed, and am persuaded that he is able to keep that which
I have committed unto him against that' – glorious – 'day'.